1,029 Backyard Birding Secrets

These tips—from bird lovers across the country—guarantee more feathered friends in your backyard!

1,029 Backyard Birding Secrets

These tips—from bird lovers across the country—guarantee more feathered friends in your backyard!

Editor: Jeff Nowak
Managing Editor: Heather Lamb
Associate Editors: Mandi Schuldt, Jean Steiner, Susan Uphill
Contributing Editor/Consulting Bird Expert: George Harrison
Editorial Assistants: Marie Brannon, Mary Ann Koebernik, Cliff Muehlenberg
Art Director: Jim Sibilski
Art Associates: Maribeth Greinke, Bonnie Ziolecki, Linda Dzik, Tom Hunt
Production: Catherine Fletcher, Ellen Lloyd
Photo Coordinator: Trudi Bellin
Publisher: Roy Reiman

Visit our Web site at *www.birdsandblooms.com* or E-mail us at *editors@birdsandblooms.com*.

Birds & Blooms Books
©2001, Reiman Publications, LLC
5400 S. 60th St., Greendale WI 53129
International Standard Book Number: 0-89821-325-8
Library of Congress Control Number: 2001135767
Printed in USA

Notice: The information in this book has been gathered from a variety of people and sources, and all efforts have been made to ensure accuracy.

Remember, not every tip is suitable for every area of the country or in every backyard.

Reiman Publications assumes no responsibility for any injuries suffered or damages or losses incurred as a result of this information. All information should be carefully studied and clearly understood before taking any action based on the information or advice in this book.

Reiman Publications does not endorse or recommend any products mentioned in this book.

For your safety, read and follow all label directions when using commercial products and call your local utilities before digging in your yard.

For additional copies of this book or information on other books, write: *Birds & Blooms* Books, P.O. Box 990, Greendale WI 53129. You can also order by phone and charge to your credit card by calling toll-free 1-800/558-1013 or visit *www.countrystore catalog.com*. Ask for item 31663 and please mention suite 4763.

Cover photo: Maslowski Photo; page 1: Bill Carter; page 2: Terry Eggers

'This Book Taught Me Many New Birding Tricks!'

FEW PEOPLE enjoy backyard birding more than I do. When I wake up each morning, I always check the feeders to see which birds beat me out of bed. Usually there's a mourning dove (all the more reason to call them *morning* doves) or a black-capped chickadee.

But even I must admit that keeping the feeders filled, the birdbath clean and still having enough energy to come up with ways to stop the pesky squirrels from devouring my offerings can be a chore. After all, this is supposed to be a relaxing hobby in my spare time.

That's why it was so much fun editing and assembling this book. It allowed me to learn from the experiences of other friendly folks who also love inviting wild birds to their backyards. But many of them are a lot more clever than I am when it comes to inventing practical and ingenious ideas for managing their backyard bird haven.

Taking Them to Task

Readers have passed on so many great ideas that sometimes I'd hurry home after editing a chapter to try one of the "secrets" they unselfishly shared.

Here's one I put to the test. Since squirrels were devouring the suet I set out for woodpeckers, I had to find a way to keep the furry critters at bay. Fortunately, I stumbled upon this tip from Bonita Laettner of Angola, New York.

To stop the determined rascals from taking over her suet cage, Bonita slips a smaller cage of suet into a larger one.

"The squirrels can't get to the cakes through this double barrier, but the birds have no trouble reaching it with their bills," she writes.

It sounded like an idea worth trying. So I purchased a larger cage and rehung the double-secure suet from the same branch in a nearby tree. Then I anxiously watched from our patio door.

Sure enough, within minutes a squirrel scurried along the branch and jumped onto the feeder. About 30 seconds later, after realizing the suet was out of its reach, the would-be raider scampered down the trunk and into my neighbor's yard, looking for an easier target.

Viola—no more pesky squirrels! And I haven't seen one on my suet

3

feeder since, thanks to Bonita.

I've found many new tips in this book that I plan on trying. Here are a few others that made me say, "Gee, why didn't I think of that?"

1. To clean hummingbird feeders, let them soak for 5 minutes in a bucket filled with warm water and a couple denture-cleaning tablets. That makes sense!

2. Place birdhouses so the entrance faces south, southeast or east—few storms come from these directions, and the morning sun will warm the house. Of course!

3. To keep the seed in tube feeders dry, pour kitty litter in the bottom, below the first feeding port, to soak up excess moisture.

Why didn't I think of that simple solution before? I would've saved a lot of seed from going bad.

Tested by My Family

Thanks to this book, the whole family can enjoy *my* favorite hobby—even our young boys!

For example, when we built a simple birdhouse (that's my son Aaron holding it) we followed the advice of Georgia Stewart from Hebron, Illinois and included a peek door to check on nesting activity. What a thrill for the kids *and* me.

And thanks to Debbie Smith of Cabot, Pennsylvania, we store our thistle in a large covered juice container. Now my son, Bennett (that's him on the left) doesn't spill a seed when he fills our tube feeders. And it stays fresher, too!

More Than 1,000 Clever Ideas

You'll find page after page of simple and helpful birding ideas like these in this practical book. It's like sitting down with more than 1,000 backyard birders who are willing to lend a hand and share their best secrets to birding success.

Plus, you'll benefit from the backyard birding expertise of *Birds & Blooms* Contributing Editor George Harrison. Besides enjoying this hobby all his life, George is a respected authority and has authored several books on the subject.

Throughout this book, we've splashed in several tried-and-true tips from George—ones he has learned in his own backyard. He al-

THUMBS UP! My sons, Bennett (left) and Aaron, have helped me test several of these fantastic birding tips—right in our own backyard.

so provides the answers to many commonly asked questions from the readers of *Birds & Blooms*.

The number of clever backyard birding ideas you'll get from this book will amaze you. Lucky for you—and me—they're not so secret anymore!

Jeff Nowak, Editor
Birds & Blooms

Contents

Chapter 9

Chapter 10

Chapter 13

Chapter 14

Chapter 1
No Vacancy

What's more rewarding than a homebuilt birdhouse decorating your backyard? How about one filled with a pair of feathered friends that have set up housekeeping?

There are about 35 North American birds in any given region that will use birdhouses to raise their young. But it takes more than four walls, a roof and a sturdy floor to attract them. It requires the proper size entrance hole and nesting cavity for the species you're trying to attract; the right location in the proper habitat; and a little bit of luck, too.

If you're hoping to hang out the "No Vacancy" sign during the spring nesting season, try some of these reader tested tips to keep your birdhouses filled to capacity.

Photo: John Gschwend Jr.

Set up several birdhouses throughout your yard. Be sure to use different-size entrance holes so different species of birds can find a house to use. (See the "Build a Better Birdhouse" chart on page 18 for appropriate entrance hole sizes.)

—*Gary Clark, Knowlton, Quebec*

If you provide pieces of string for birds during nesting season, remember to cut them into sections only a couple inches long so birds don't get tangled in the threads.

—*Eleanor Alford*
Chesapeake, Virginia

Dad always said wrens wouldn't nest in a birdhouse if they can see other wrens (below). So I'm always careful to place my wren houses out of sight of each other.

—*Nona Fleach, Belmont, Wisconsin*

Mary Clay

> ### IT'S A FACT...
> Homes for Birds Week is usually scheduled for the fourth week in February. This is a good time to clean out, fix up and put up homes for backyard birds.

Carolina wrens are always welcome in my yard—they eat lots of pesky insects. To encourage them to nest here, I place a variety of containers that are about the size of a 1-gallon milk jug around my yard. (Carolina wrens aren't picky when choosing nesting cavities as long as they're roomy.) They've inhabited a swimming pool skimmer, an empty flowerpot, a hanging Styrofoam ice chest and an old bookcase.

—*Rebecca King*
Burlison, Tennessee

Many species of birds will not nest next to each other. But bluebirds and tree swallows are a different story.

I place two bluebird houses 15 feet away from each other. That way the bluebirds get one nest box and tree swallows often willingly inhabit the other. They coexist harmoniously, yet other "pests" like house sparrows stay away.

—*Shirley Barribeau*
Goodman, Wisconsin

I place a birdhouse in the center of our large garden because the birds eat many unwanted bugs. But I didn't want to work around a large mounting post, so I built a teepee structure from four metal poles. I tied them together at the top, evenly

spaced the legs and hung a birdhouse in the center. It's a great way to create a moveable birdhouse.
—*Louise Martin*
Memphis, Missouri

Leave birdhouses up all year. Clean them in late fall and spray the inside of the birdhouse with a strong stream of water.
—*Sue Hensley*
Lenoir City, Tennessee

We've increased the number of house finches nesting in our yard by wiring small strawberry baskets in the corners of the awnings on our house. We put up four baskets one year and watched 38 house finches fledge from the nests. During winter, some finches even roost in them. —*Doris Bartel*
Hillsboro, Kansas

Avoid pruning branches from the trees in your yard. This provides more nesting cover.

Bluebirds and ground feeders, like mourning doves, also use this cover for protection and often select low-growing perches (6 to 15 feet from the ground) as a place to watch for their next meal. I also leave some dead branches for the birds, too.
—*James Thiessen*
Hodgson, Manitoba

Mount birdhouses on 4-inch PVC pipe that's about 8 feet long. The slippery surface of the post prevents snakes, cats and other predators from disturbing the nests. A 4-inch-diameter toilet flange mounted to the base of the birdhouse is perfect for attaching it to the top of the pipe. —*Sherry and Dean Johnson*
West Fargo, North Dakota

All my birdhouses (like the one above) have an easy-open door so I can periodically check on the activity in the nest box.
—*Georgia Stewart, Hebron, Illinois*

Here's a way to protect nests that are out in the open. A pair of mourning doves built a nest in our yard that wasn't very sheltered, so my husband secured an umbrella to a branch above it. It worked perfectly, keeping the birds cool and protected from the elements.
—*Peggy Bell, Fresno, California*

Long-handled dipper gourds (like the ones I grew above) are the best ones for making birdhouses.
—*Glenn Burkhalter*
Laceys Springs, Alabama

I secure nest boxes to trees by wrapping bungee cords around the trunks. It looks nice, holds firmly and doesn't damage the tree like nails do. Plus, once nesting season is over, I can remove the boxes and store them until next year.
—*Clyde Keeler, Lanesville, Indiana*

Birds in my yard only inhabit empty birdhouses. So I clean mine in September. If the houses aren't kept clean, parasites may invade them.
—*Edward Scott*
Crittenden, Kentucky

After I brush my dog, I save the excess hair for the spring nesting season. I place the fur and short lengths of yarn throughout my yard, then watch birds collect the material for their nests. —*Cathlyn Ramsey*
Wichita, Kansas

Place an inch of clean cedar shavings in the bottom of birdhouses to provide extra cushioning. Birds incorporate the shavings into their nests. —*Betsy Rogers*
Puyallup, Washington

ASK GEORGE
Birds frequently visit my bird feeders, but they ignore the birdhouses I have fastened to trees on the perimeter of a wooded area. What do I need to do to entice birds to use them?
—*Shirley Walter*
Lancaster, New York

George: You must locate birdhouses in habitat suitable for the birds you're trying to attract. The house must also be built with those kinds of birds in mind—different species need different-size houses and entrance holes, and the houses must be located at a proper height.

For more detailed information, turn to page 18 and review the "Build a Better Birdhouse" chart.

Save chicken or duck feathers and put them out on a calm spring day. Then watch the birds swoop down and collect them for their nests. —*Verna Olson Fargo, North Dakota*

IT'S A FACT...
Cavity-nesting birds usually lay white eggs because there's no need for camouflage.

Collect fallen branches and make a neat pile for birds. They not only use the pile for protection, but they also find tiny branches in it for nest building. —*Gary Clark Knowlton, Quebec*

I paint "attraction dots" (pictured above) on each side of my bluebird houses. The 1-1/2-inch black circles look like entrance holes and are intended to catch the bluebirds' attention as they scout for places to raise their young. —*Marcia Hoepfner Metamora, Illinois*

I love coffee and have dozens of empty 3-pound cans lying around. I found bluebirds think these cans

make excellent houses. Simply drill or cut a 1-1/2-inch hole in the plastic lid and mount the house to a tree through the can's metal bottom. To clean, simply remove the plastic lid and scoop out the nest remnants. Be sure to place these houses in the shade to keep the sun from heating the metal surface. —*Sue McKee Iuka, Mississippi*

Encourage barn swallows to nest on barn beams by nailing a 3-inch-long scrap of wood to the beam (horizontally) about 4 inches below the ceiling. This gives them a foundation for their mud nests. —*Chriss Stutzman, Navarre, Ohio*

We're landlords of 144 purple martin gourd houses. One year we had problems with parasites infesting the nests. But quick thinking prevented a repeat occurrence.

We sprinkled cedar shavings (about 1 to 2 inches deep) in the houses. The cedar is a chemical-free way to repel the pests. —*Sandra Cearley Copperhill, Tennessee*

Birdhouses don't mix with busy roads. I place mine along seldom-traveled roads in our backyard and pasture to prevent unfortunate accidents. —*John Keller Piedmont, Ohio*

I grow calabash gourds and make them into purple martin houses. Let them completely dry (they take 4 to 6 months to dry out), then remove the outer skin by soaking and scrubbing them. Drill four drainage holes in the bottom of each gourd, then bore the main entrance hole (2-1/2 inches) in the side. Soak them in a wood preservative or paint them with a white outdoor paint to protect them from the weather.

Martins are fussy about location of the houses, so I hang the gourds about 14 feet high in an open yard. Most of the birds return year after year. —*Franklin Bidinger Lawrence, Kansas*

Attach an old television antenna to the top of a purple martin house. It won't improve television reception, but the birds love to perch on it. —*Wendell Obermeier Charles City, Iowa*

When a large tree in my backyard (pictured below) had to be cut down, I left the trunk and a few sturdy branches for mounting birdhouses. I even attached some to the trunk. —*Jacque Hodson, Ackworth, Iowa*

RP Photo

Paint purple martin houses white (like above) because it reflects the sun's rays and keeps the houses cooler. I also place the entrance holes in different locations in each gourd so the martins can determine which house is theirs.—*Victor Stoll Finger, Tennessee*

Fill suet cages with nesting materials like dryer lint, yarn, pet hair and cotton balls. —*Michaeline Pearson Lehighton, Pennsylvania*

Want to make your own gourd birdhouse? Try these tips from gourd grower Claude Wade of Franklin, Indiana:

- Gourds can take between 3 months to a year to completely dry. Dry them on several layers of newspaper in a warm place or hang from a tree or deck in a sunny place.
- Mold might appear on gourds as they dry. This is natural, so don't throw the gourds away. However, if a gourd becomes soft or wrinkled, toss it out immediately.
- Gourds are completely dry when you can hear the seeds rattling inside when you shake them. Now it's time to scrub them with a stainless steel pad in warm soapy water to remove the mold.
- Drill appropriate-size entrance holes (see chart on page 18) for the cavity-nesting birds you'd like to attract. Remove the seeds through the hole, using the handle of a wooden spoon or a wire coat hanger. Holes should be 1-1/4 inches for house

Bonnie Nance

wrens, 1-1/2 inches for bluebirds and 2-1/2 inches for purple martins. Always add several small holes at the bottom for drainage.

Add a 1/2-inch-tall platform made of hardware cloth inside each nest box to keep nesting material from touching the floor. Because the nests are raised, the houses don't attract flies that lay eggs in damp places. *—Debbi Piro Vintondale, Pennsylvania*

A week before orioles are due back to our area, I place small tuna cans filled with grape jelly on our deck rails. I also set out string for them to use in their pouch-shaped nests. Not only do these birds love the treats, but gray catbirds and red-bellied woodpeckers also enjoy them. *—Bev Kalsem, Madrid, Iowa*

Want to help nesting wrens or bluebirds feed their young? Buy wax worms or mealworms from a local bait shop and set a few on a nearby tray feeder. Then watch the parents snatch up the worms and take them to their chicks.
—Jerilyn Veltus Neillsville, Wisconsin

Here are a few tips to attract nesting bluebirds to your yard:
- Provide plenty of clean water in a nearby birdbath.
- Bluebirds appreciate a host of berry trees and shrubs. Keep two nest boxes near each other—one for bluebirds and the other for tree swallows.
- Because bluebirds build new nests for each brood, clean out the old one after the young leave. This encourages a second and third nest in the same house during a single nesting season.

—*Bernice Maddux*
Weatherford, Texas

Hubert Brandenburg

I build bluebird houses with entrance slots instead of holes. The slot measures the width of the front board and is 1-1/8 inches high. Starlings and sparrows won't attempt to enter the slotted entrance. And it gives the bluebirds a chance to escape from predators if necessary.

—*Bill Shumway*
Amherst, Massachusetts

The secret to attracting lots of nesting birds is offering variety. Plant different kinds of flowers, shrubs and trees, and keep your birdbath sparkling clean.

—*Audrey Anderson*
Boyceville, Wisconsin

Keep nest boxes free of bees and wasps by rubbing a bar of soap on the interior roof of the box. The birds can't smell it and will have a bug-free home. —*Fred Sahl*
Church Road, Virginia

Birdhouse entrance holes should face south because storms usually don't come from that direction. —*Chriss Stutzman*
Navarre, Ohio

Purple martins prefer birdhouses with bright interiors. So I spray their houses with turpentine to kill any bird lice. Then I paint the inside with silver-colored paint. This also seems to deter starlings that might be interested in the residence.

—*A.J. Stanisich*
Eveleth, Minnesota

Hang strawberry baskets under roof and porch eaves during nesting season. Place a few small twigs in the baskets and wait to see which birds nest in them. —*Anna Miller*
Goshen, Indiana

IT'S A FACT...
Parents brood, or cover, young birds to protect them from rain, cold and hot sun.

Avoid interfering with young birds that appear to be orphaned. Although we want to ensure the safety of all birds raised in our backyards, the parents often are nearby, watching over their young that have fledged.

If a young bird is injured, call a local wildlife rehabilitation center licensed to care for wild birds.
—*Diana Kidd, Alexandria, Virginia*

Holly Byrne

Near one of our most popular birdhouses, we mount a box filled with soft colorful items like feathers, cotton and strips of unused fabric. The birds know to stop at the bright box for nesting materials.
—*John and Vi Howe*
Miles City, Montana

Convert bluebird houses into bed-and-breakfasts by attaching small feeding dishes to the tops of the post for mealworms, commercially produced bluebird food and raisins. The bluebirds can't resist nesting in our yard because of these extra offerings.
—*Donald Thalacker*
Palmyra, Virginia

Save quilt trimmings for spring when the birds are collecting nesting material. I leave clusters of the soft yarn throughout my yard. It's a good way to recycle. —*Kathy Kermen*
Yreka, California

An old satellite dish makes the perfect hanger for purple martin gourd houses. My husband, Robert, recycled our old dish by mounting it so it looks like an umbrella atop an 18-foot post sunk 2 feet into the ground. At the top, he created a pulley system that attaches to the dish, allowing him to raise and lower it to clean out the gourds in fall.
—*Rose Mitchell*
Gibsonville, North Carolina

ASK GEORGE

I've read that it's not good to scatter clothes dryer lint for nesting material because it will become matted when wet. Is this true? —*Delores Paul*
Edina, Minnesota

George: It's true that clothes dryer lint will become matted when wet, but birds will not use any material in their nests that's harmful to their offspring. If you're still concerned, try offering cotton yarn, string and hair instead.

Gary W. Carter

Some birds (like the American robins above) love our evergreens during nesting season. The bigger and denser, the better place for them to build a nest. Their favorite nesting trees in my yard are blue spruce, Douglas fir and dwarf Alberta spruce.   —*Tina Jacobs*
Wantage, New Jersey

To keep starlings from nesting in my martin houses, I don't make round entrance holes. Instead, I cut half-circle holes. (For more information, see the box below.) Starlings can't enter this type of hole.
—*Rachel Gingerich*
Bloomfield, Iowa

Starlings a Problem for Your Martins? Lock Them Out with This Half-a-Hole

IF YOU'VE BEEN TRYING to attract purple martins to your backyard, but pesky European starlings are keeping them from moving into the neighborhood, you may want to give this starling-resistant entrance hole a try.

The half-a-hole has been tested throughout North America for several years and has proven to be successful on both purple martin houses and gourds. They work because starlings are too large to fit their bodies into the narrow entrance.

The height of the hole (1-3/16 inches) is extremely critical to making the entrance work. A hair too big and starlings will get in. A hair too small and the martins will be locked out.

To make the entrance hole easier to cut with a saber saw, locate it flush with the floor. That way you can start cutting from the bottom edge of each entrance door.

If you're attempting to attract purple martins to your yard for the first time, the Purple Martin Conservation Association recommends using these holes *only* in the upper compartments. If they work, simply switch the doors to the lower compartments to match before the martins return from their winter grounds the next spring.

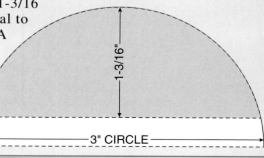

1-3/16"

3" CIRCLE

By George... A wooden purple martin house is the best option in the South because the compartments remain relatively cool. Be sure all martin houses are well ventilated and painted white to reflect heat.

—George Harrison
Contributing Editor

RP Photo

Rather than removing a dead tree, cut off any dangerous branches and leave the substantial trunk for woodpeckers to use as a nesting and feeding site. These birds are continually losing their natural habitat. *—Louaine Leisching*
Hendersonville, North Carolina

The quickest way to attract martins to a man-made purple martin apartment is to attach gourd houses below or near it. The martins fight to claim the gourds first. Once they're occupied, the rest settle for a compartment in the house.

—Carol Nash
Hamilton, New Jersey

Use elongated entrance holes in your birdhouses. These allow birds to easily bring small twigs into the nesting cavity. *—Jack Hall*
Mahomet, Illinois

By the time wrens arrived in spring, all our birdhouses were filled with bluebirds and swallows. So I quickly made nesting shelters for them from laundry detergent bottles.

I thoroughly cleaned them and cut off the protruding spout. Then I inserted a small wooden dowel below the spout as a perch and cut vent holes in the sides of the container. The wrens took up residence within a few days. *—Geraldine Bartel*
Fremont, Wisconsin

Robins often nest in the woven baskets I mount outside. Simply turn them on their side and attach them to a wall with a few screws.

Locate them under an overhang so the birds are protected from the elements. *—Connie Moore*
Medway, Ohio

Birdhouse Building Guideline

SPECIES	DIMENSIONS	HOLE	PLACEMENT	COLOR	NOTES
Eastern bluebird	5" x 5" x 8"h.	1-1/2" centered 6" above floor	5-10' high in the open; sunny area	light earth tones	likes open areas, especially facing a field
Tree swallow	5" x 5" x 6"h.	1-1/2" centered 4" above floor	5-8' high in the open; 50-100% sun	light earth tones or gray	within 2 miles of pond or lake
Purple martin	multiple apts. 6" x 6" x 6" ea.	2-1/2" hole 2-1/4" above floor	15-20' high in the open	white	open yard without tall trees; near water
Tufted titmouse	4" x 4" x 8"h.	1-1/4"	4-10' high	light earth tones	prefers to live in or near woods
Chickadee	4" x 4" x 8"h. or 5" x 5" base	1-1/8" centered 6" above floor	4-8' high	light earth tones	small tree thicket
Nuthatch	4" x 4" x 10"h.	1-1/4" centered 7-1/2" above floor	12-25' high on tree trunk	bark-covered or natural	
House wren	4" x 4" x 8"h. or 4" x 6" base	1" centered 6" above floor	5-10' high on post or hung in tree	light earth tones or white	may fill nest boxes with "dummy" nests
Northern flicker	7" x 7" x 18"h.	2-1/2" centered 14" above floor	8-20' high	light earth tones	put 4" sawdust inside for nesting
Downy woodpecker	4" x 4" x 10"h.	1-1/4" centered 7-1/2" above floor	12-25' high on tree trunk	simulate natural cavity	prefers own excavation; provide sawdust
Red-headed woodpecker	6" x 6" x 15"h.	2" centered 6-8" above floor	8-20' high on post or tree trunk	simulate natural cavity	needs sawdust for nesting
Wood duck	10" x 10" x 24"h.	4" x 3" elliptical 20" above floor	2-5' high on post over water, or 12-40' high on tree facing water	light earth tones or natural	needs 3-4" of sawdust or shavings for nesting
American kestrel	10" x 10" x 24"h.	4" x 3" elliptical 20" above floor	12-40' high on post or tree trunk	light earth tones or natural	needs open approach on edge of woodlot or in isolated tree
Screech owl	10" x 10" x 24"h.	4" x 3" elliptical 20" above floor	2-5' high on post over water, or 12-40' high on tree	light earth tones or natural	prefers open woods or edge of woodlot
NESTING SHELVES					
American robin	6" x 6" x 8"h.	none—needs roof for rain protection	on side of building or arbor or in tree	light earth tones or wood	use is irregular
Barn swallow	6" x 6" x 8"h.	none—does not need roof	under eaves of building	light earth tones or wood	prefers barns or outbuildings
Phoebe	6" x 6" x 8"h.	none—does not need roof	under eaves of building	light earth tones or wood	prefers water nearby

Note: With the exception of wrens, birds generally do not tolerate swaying birdhouses. Birdhouses should be firmly anchored to a post, a tree or the side of a building.

Source: *Garden Birds of America* by George H. Harrison. Willow Creek Press, 1996.

*F*rom hubcaps to plastic milk jugs, just about anything can be fashioned into a fantastic feeder. Just make sure there's plenty of birdseed, suet or sugar water to satisfy your feathered friends.

We've collected plenty of clever reader ideas to create pro-ductive bird feeders that are the busiest "restaurants" in the neigh-borhood. And to keep your clien-tele of the feathered variety, we've also included several reader sug-gestions that will help reserve your establishments exclusively for the birds.

Photo: J.C. Miller

This homemade feeder (above) hangs from a wire strung between two trees. A wooden dowel on each side serves as a perch, and the tray is open on the sides to let rainwater drain. Extra seed does fall through these openings as well, giving ground feeders a chance to eat, too.

—*Eugene Westley*
Lemon Springs, North Carolina

I hang a suet cage at the edge of our yard and attach orange slices to it in spring. This not only attracts suet-eating birds, but also brings in beautiful Baltimore orioles.

—*Diane Gratton*
Knowlton, Quebec

I attach a plastic squirrel baffle to my feeder post, fastening it upside down so it catches falling birdseed. This saves me lots of weeding time, plus it provides birds with more places to perch because they eat from the baffle, too.

To keep the seed from getting moldy, drill a few 1/8-inch holes in the bottom of the baffle for drainage.

—*Linda Gregg*
Grand Rapids, Michigan

Several years ago, we mount[ed] few simple tray feeders along deck railing. They're inexpens and unobtrusive. But the best is they attract tons of birds, bring them close to the house so we watch them from inside.

We've come up with a sim way to mount these tray feeder the deck rail so they can easily removed for cleaning. Just drill 1/2-inch holes into the base of e feeder. Then set the feeder on rail where you'd like it mount Using the predrilled holes a guide, drill two more correspond 1/2-inch holes into the deck r making each one about 1 inch de

Cut a 1/2-inch dowel into 1- inch lengths, and glue the dowels to the holes in the railing. Then s ply slip the feeder onto the dow If wind is a problem in your ar as it is in mine, I suggest drillin 1/8-inch hole through the top one of the dowels. Then slip a nai piece of wire through it to keep feeders from falling off the rail.

—*Karen Jo*
Sebastopol, Califor

I make bird feeders from 2-liter plastic soda bottles. Simply cut a large opening in the side of the bottle, as pictured in the diagram at right. Fill the bottle with seed up to the opening, and hang the bottle from a string or wire.

—*Patricia Carty*
Nashville, Tennessee

I attach terra-cotta flowerpot saucers to posts around my deck and fill them with birdseed. It's an easy and inexpensive way to serve all of my feathered friends.
—*Sheryl Neal*
Carrollton, Ohio

We provide three tube-style thistle feeders exclusively designed for American goldfinches. These feeders have perches *above* the feeding ports, so the finches have to eat upside down. The goldfinches are the only birds in our yard that have mastered the trick! —*Virginia Jensen*
Millington, Michigan

Serve dried corncobs to wildlife by driving a large nail halfway into the top of a post. Cut the head off with a bolt cutter and spear the ear of corn onto the spike.
—*Chriss Stutzman, Navarre, Ohio*

Birdseed doesn't spoil in my yard—I've found an inexpensive way to protect it from moisture.

Simply attach a piece of Plexiglas above tray-style feeders (pictured below left). This allows the birds to see what's in the feeder while keeping the seed dry. It also makes my feeders a popular hangout on a rainy day. Remember to use a piece that's about an inch wider and longer than the feeder. —*Rebecca King*
Burlison, Tennessee

Since my children outgrew their swing set, I created a feeding station by hanging feeders from the frame. It's now equipped with a variety of feeders hung from varying lengths of wire. —*Jill Hersch*
Ayr, North Dakota

Solve the problem of spilled seed under your bird feeder by using a "holey" pizza pan. My husband, Stan, bored a hole the size of the feeder pole in the center of the pan. Then he secured it with a hose clamp directly beneath the feeder. The tiny holes allow for drainage, and the birds have a terrific second place to feed from. —*Jayne Bell*
Greenwood, South Carolina

bles a narrow trough. Tie strings through each end of the trough, hang it from a tree branch and fill it with seed. The feeders look great, and the birds love them.   —*Nancy Burns*
Fredericksburg, Texas

To keep the seed in my tube feeders dry, I pour plain kitty litter in the bottom about 1 inch below the first feeding port. This saves me from wasting seed the birds can't reach anyway and soaks up moisture accumulated in the feeder.
—*Nancy Sterling*
Butler, Pennsylvania

Pizza pans solved the problem of sunflower seeds falling to the ground beneath my feeder.

I screwed the pans (the "crispy crust" kind with hundreds of tiny holes in them) to the bottom of my feeder. They keep spilled seed from falling to the ground and allow wet seed to dry quickly.

The pans also offer a roomy feeding surface for the birds.
—*Daisy Ballard, Purcell, Oklahoma*

Since we only visit our campsite on the weekends, we needed a feeder that could hold a week's worth of seed. My husband crafted this feeder (above) that holds 5 gallons of birdseed. Its two copper roofs deflect the rain, and the wide base accommodates many birds.
—*Carla Sherack*
Red Wing, Minnesota

I use wire coat hangers to hang feeders. Simply straighten them and cut them to the length you need. Then bend the ends into hook shapes, one to hold the feeder and one to hang from a branch. Now, just lift to remove for cleaning or refilling.
—*June Smith, Woodruff, Wisconsin*

Two simple feeders can be made from a length of dead tree limb. Just cut the limb in half lengthwise and hollow out the center until it resem-

If seed falls from your feeder because the ports are too large, place a piece of duct tape over one quarter or one half of the hole. It works like a charm.   —*Mary Gilliland*
Marion, Iowa

IT'S A FACT...
To discourage pigeons, use hanging tube feeders and sunflower seeds with the hulls on.

RP Photo

One of my favorite crafts is making dried wreaths for my feathered friends (above). I collect lots of seed heads in late summer, like sunflowers, purple coneflowers, bromegrass and tassel flower. I'll even gather some crab apples. Once the flowers and fruits have dried, wire them to a grapevine or straw wreath, making sure all the ends are tucked deep into the wreath so they don't hurt the birds. —*Sharon Challand Malta, Illinois*

To make a portable feeder, attach a feeder to a post anchored in a 5-gallon bucket filled with soil. You can plant flowers in the soil or allow it to catch fallen seed.
—*Carol Doenges, Coldwater, Ohio*

To keep the birds at our weekend home well fed throughout the week, we've created an enormous feeder, so the food is flowing even when we're not there.

We built a platform high enough so deer can't reach it. Then we fastened a 25-gallon galvanized steel garbage can to the platform and drilled several tiny feeding ports a couple inches above the bottom of the can. Now we can rest easy knowing our birds have lots of seed when we're gone. —*Naomi Mayhew Waterford, Michigan*

Hardwood logs make great suet feeders. Select ones that are 3 to 4 inches in diameter and about 1 foot long. Drill holes that are 1-1/2 inches deep and wide and insert 1/4-inch dowels below the feeding ports. Fill each hole with a suet mix. (To make your own suet, see the "Award-Winning Recipes" chapter beginning on page 55).
—*Sandy Szot-Burmeister New London, Wisconsin*

Feeders don't have to be fancy to attract lots of birds. Groups of evening grosbeaks visit my backyard when I set out a simple pie plate filled with sunflower seeds atop a kitchen stool. What's most important is to provide the proper seed and keep it coming!
—*Marcy Cella, L'Anse, Michigan*

When I replaced my window screens, I converted some into tray feeders (below). I placed four clay

pots on the ground, and set the frame of the screen on top of them. Chipmunks, squirrels and birds all visit this tray feeder that keeps the seed dry. —*"Ducky" Conniff Lewiston, Minnesota*

I make a transparent window feeder using a suction-cup hook and a 2-liter soda bottle. Cut the bottle as shown in the diagram at right and poke a hole in the back,  so it can hang from the suction cup. Fasten it to the window and fill with seed. You'll see backyard birds closer than ever before. —*Alan McIver Egg Harbor Township, New Jersey*

We built a terrific feeding station that attracts lots of different birds  (pictured at left). The large roof provides them with an ideal spot to land. And a metal hanging bracket attached to the feeder gives us a place to hang a thistle feeder for finches. Any spilled thistle doesn't go to waste—the roof catches most of it, and it's quickly eaten.
—*Barb and Kent Mitchell St. Charles, Minnesota*

My mesh thistle feeder constantly needed refilling. To solve the problem, I fill a large plastic juice bottle with the seed and attach the mesh bag to the mouth of the bottle with a strong rubber band. Then I hang it upside down so it refills the bag automatically. Even though American goldfinches feverishly work to empty it, I only refill the thistle seed once a week.
—*Carol Makosky Webster, Wisconsin*

Years ago, I noticed birds were pecking at jack-o'-lanterns that had been left from Halloween. Now I use our carved pumpkins as feeders by enlarging the carved opening and filling it with birdseed. Mourning doves and other ground-feeding birds really love the seeds…and the pumpkin.
—*Phyllis Pottorff-Albrecht Broomfield, Colorado*

My brother, Tom, created a simple feeder tray from an old piece of farm equipment. He attached a disk blade to a pipe and attached the pipe vertically to a steel fence post. It's a good idea to drill a couple of holes in the disk for adequate drainage.
—*Eva Wilson, Topeka, Kansas*

To prolong the life of wooden bird feeders, drill a few small holes in the area of the floor that's exposed to the elements. This allows the floor and seed on it to dry more quickly after a rain, which helps keep the wood from rotting.
—*Marian Ducrest Broussard, Louisiana*

To create a mobile bird feeder, fill a large ceramic flowerpot with concrete and stick the bird feeder pole into the concrete. Now I can move it wherever I wish.
—*Sam Kent West Caldwell, New Jersey*

I live in a relatively new suburb of Denver, so the young trees in my yard aren't big enough to offer birds much protection. However, I've found a way to bring them in—I hang mesh bags (the kind that potatoes and onions are packaged in) from one of the larger trees in my yard and fill them with grapes. The American robins (at left) and finches now seem to congregate in this tree and appear to love the treats. —*Kristin Forrest Aurora, Colorado*

Here's a quick way to hang feeders from trees. Tie a heavy metal nut to the end of a length of string or twine and toss it over a strong branch. Slip the opposite end of the string through the nut and pull tight. Then tie on a spring-loaded swivel hook (like the kind used on most pet leashes) and hang the feeder. —*Chris King Burlington, Iowa*

My dad builds bird feeders from just about anything he finds around the house. This one (pictured below) works especially well.

Begin with a piece of 4-inch PVC plumbing pipe (lengths can vary) and drill 1-3/4-inch evenly spaced holes using a saber saw.

Remove the top portion of 1/2-gallon milk jugs (as shown at far right)—one for every feeding port. Attach each plastic top to the PVC pipe with one screw as shown.

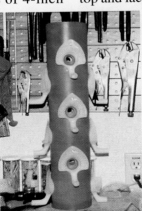

Then fasten recycled plastic tops from a bucket or other container (at least 4 inches in diameter) to both ends of the pipe. To do this, drill a hole in the center of each plastic top and lace a string (which will also be used for hanging) through the hole. Fill the pipe with birdseed and let your feathered friends dine in style.

—*Phil Flemming Mocksville, North Carolina*

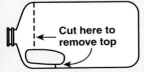

Cut here to remove top

critters to slip off. If they don't, their weight lowers the dome over the feeding tray so the critters can't get to the food. It's quite effective.

—*Helen Nealon*
Scranton, Pennsylvania

Mailboxes make excellent feeders that keep the seed protected from the wind and rain. I just leave the door open and lock it in place with metal strapping (above). —*Donna Kromm Calgary, Alberta*

My favorite feeder really is 100% squirrel proof. A lightweight spring supports a dome cover over the feeding tray, which usually causes the

Like others, I have a simple log feeder that I fill with suet. But without perches, only woodpeckers feed from it. So I inserted corncob holders below each feeding port to give other birds a place to perch and enjoy the treat. —*Gordon Raymond Miramichi, New Brunswick*

Instead of throwing away old baskets, I nail them to my porch railing and fill them with peanuts and sunflower seeds. The birds and squirrels share these treats.

—*Annette MacDonald*
Hampton, Ontario

ASK GEORGE

Why do birds seem to feed in frenzies? Often, my feeders are vacant for hours at a time...then crowded with cardinals, chickadees and nuthatches all at once. Why don't the birds eat at

different times so there's less competition for the food?
—*Alex Grieves, Topeka, Kansas*

George: Birds do travel and feed in groups with other birds, particularly in the winter. That's because the more eyes there are to search, the more likely they are to find food. Also, there's safety in numbers—if many birds are present, predators are less likely to attack.

Birds also tend to feed in "frenzies" before a storm because they sense the coming low pressure and feed heavily in preparation for bad weather.

To convince yellow-bellied sapsuckers to stop drilling holes in my pecan tree for sap and insects, I developed a simple grape jelly feeder for them.

I cut a small hole at the bottom edge of a clear 35mm plastic film container that's just big enough for the jelly to ooze out. Then I tacked it to the tree in a protected spot. The sapsuckers adore this special treat. —*Sue Mozelle*
Ridgeland, Mississippi

I make inexpensive tray feeders from plastic bedding-plant flats. The flats are approximately 11 inches x 16 inches.

I lay a piece of window screen with the same dimensions into the bottom of the flat and loosely sew it in place with fishing line. Then I punch a hole in the top corners of the flat and attach a 16-inch length of string or chain to each corner. I'll connect the string or chains on each narrow end with a metal ring and hang them from my porch or clothesline. —*Lyda Henson*
Locust Grove, Oklahoma

My father builds seed catchers for our hanging feeders. He constructs a wooden frame that is 3 inches larger than the base of the feeder and

My most visited feeder is a simple 15-inch-long tree limb with eight 3/4-inch holes bored about 3/4 inch deep. I mix peanut butter with cornmeal and press it into the holes. Nuthatches, chickadees, woodpeckers, juncos and house finches love the treat.
—*Doris Winter*
LeSueur, Minnesota

attaches wire screen to the bottom so dropped seed dries quickly. Then he chains the seed catchers to the bottom of the feeders (pictured below left). This not only keeps unwanted seed off the ground, it also increases the birds' feeding area.
—*Kim Justice, Vero Beach, Florida*

We converted an old circular clothesline frame into a bird-feeding station. Each year we add more feeders to the collection, which brings more and more birds to our backyard. —*Janez Tracy*
Robinson, Illinois

If you're housebound, you don't have to give up feeding the birds. Ask someone to place a feeder within arm's reach of an easy-to-open window. We suspended a feeder from the eaves outside our kitchen window. Now we simply open the window and fill the feeder with a long-handled spoon.
—*Rita and Jerry Schears*
Waupun, Wisconsin

Instead of cutting down a tree in our backyard, we chopped off the top half and left a flat surface for us to mount a critter feeder (at left). Its rustic look resembles something constructed by the Swiss Family Robinson and serves both squirrels and birds. Surprisingly, they coexist in harmony.
—*Lois Butler*
Largo, Florida

I offer the birds flower heads that have gone to seed with this easy-to-make feeder. Begin with a 3-foot section of chicken wire. Roll it lengthwise into a cylinder and hold

---

IT'S A FACT... Buy wild birdseed in the largest bag you can safely handle and store. It'll save you a lot of money.

---

it together with wire. (Be careful—you don't want any sharp edges sticking out that may injure the birds.) Attach it to a stake or hang it from a branch.

Then poke the stems of cut flower heads through the cylinder and insert a few sticks for the birds to use as perches. It's fun to watch your feathered friends enjoy this all-natural treat.
—*Melvin Abels*
Pontiac, Illinois

Set a funnel upside down inside an empty feeder before filling it with seed. This forces the seed to flow to the feeding ports rather than getting stuck in the center.
—*Theresa Denby*
Gloucester, Virginia

Our homemade thistle feeder is a hit with American goldfinches. Just sew nylon mesh cloth into 10-inch-long tubes. Sew one end closed, but leave the other open for easy refilling. Once filled, tie the open end shut and hang it from a tree branch. —*Josephine McKinney*
Rockwood, Tennessee

A cheap but highly visited feeder can be made from a wire hanger, corncob and peanut butter and birdseed. Simply cut the straight part of the hanger 4 inches longer than the corncob. Bend a small loop in one end of the hanger to hook over a tree branch. Then insert the wire into the corncob. Cover the cob with peanut butter and roll it in birdseed. The entire feeder (except the hanger) is edible!
—*Carolyn Retey*
Sparr, Florida

I mount plastic garbage can covers over my tray-style bird feeders. This keeps the seed dry, preventing it from molding or germinating.
—*Gladys Pulak, Calgary, Alberta*

Now that my children are grown, the yard gym serves a different purpose. Potted plants, feeders, a water dish and suet baskets now hang from the monkey bars, while sunflowers, coneflowers, marigolds and cosmos grow below it (see photo at right). What a practical use for something that was sitting idle. —*Ruth Yoder Newtown Square, Pennsylvania*

els through the jug, placing one on each side of the container's handle. Cut a 3/8-inch x 1/2-inch opening where indicated in the jug's handle as a feeding port. Drill a couple of 1/16-inch holes in the cap for drainage. Use a funnel to fill with sunflower seeds and hang upside down. Bon appetite! —*Roe Snyder Herculaneum, Missouri*

A 1-gallon milk container really can be fashioned into a perfect bird feeder. Here's how to make one:

Poke or drill holes on opposite corners about an inch from the bottom and insert a 1/4-inch wooden dowel (see diagram at right). Wrap wire or tie a string to the dowel to make the feeder's hanger.

Insert two more 1/4-inch dow-

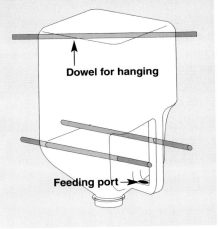

Dowel for hanging

Feeding port →

There's no need to purchase expensive bird feeders when you can build one for less than $5. Here's one of my homemade feeders (below) that works like a million bucks!

I simply converted a plastic "chip-and-dip" container and cover and a plastic vase into an attractive feeder. I first  drilled several small holes through the bottom container to help with drainage. Then I drilled slightly larger holes through the center of all three pieces. I also made a few large holes near the vase's lip for the seed to flow from.

To assemble, place the vase upside down on the container with the lid above the vase. All three pieces are held together with a piece of rope or twine from which it's hung (tie a knot in the bottom end of the rope). Simply slide the vase up the rope, turn over and fill with seed. Then place the base over the vase, pull the rope so the knot is tight against the container and turn it over again. You're ready to feed the birds for the cost of chicken feed.

—*Norma Leib*
Los Ojos, New Mexico

Assemble a quick tray feeder by using a piece of nylon window screen in a large embroidery hoop. Trim off the excess screen and attach four pieces of heavy string to the hoop.

Hang it upside down so the hoop forms a lip around the edge, which will keep the seed from falling to the ground.
—*Gladys Smith*
Greenleaf, Idaho

I fill old muffin tins with suet and nail them to scrap lumber. This way, the birds can eat right out of the tins and they won't tip over.
—*Ellen Yoder, Plain City, Ohio*

I hang feeders from cable and pulley devices. When they need filling, just release the cable and lower the feeders. Then I'll raise them to a height out of the reach of most ground predators.
—*Mary Ann Butler, Hope, Maine*

Due to arthritis, it was difficult for me to reach the bird feeders hanging from trees in my backyard. So now I hang them lower by using bungee cords (above). Filling feeders is much less painful.
—*Marjorie Riggio*
Green Bay, Wisconsin

• Landscape around the feeder with crushed stone, creating a ground-feeding area (at left), or start a garden for the seeds to grow wild.

• Offer suet instead of seed.

—*Penny Wessenauer*
Santa Clarita, California

We like to provide seed on our concrete patio for ground-feeding birds, but didn't want the seed to blow around. So my husband took an old leaky garden hose and formed a small circle with it. Now when we spread some birdseed within the circle, it stays put.

—*Rogene Carlyle*
North Platte, Nebraska

An easy and inexpensive bird-feeding tower can be made from concrete cinder blocks. Stack the blocks with the holes facing out. Then place different types of bird-seed in each compartment. You can create your own design. I added a large pan to the top of my stack that serves as a birdbath. —*Sue Sayre*
Milan, Missouri

I asked *Birds & Blooms* readers for some tips to keep seeds from sprouting below my feeders. Here are some of their answers:

• Use a wet-dry vacuum or lawn-mower with a bag attachment to remove fallen hulls and seeds.

ASK GEORGE

How can I keep starlings off my wire-basket suet feeders? They monopolize the feeders and don't give other birds a chance to eat. —*Teresa Neely*
Knoxville, Tennessee

George: To discourage starlings, mount the suet feeder under a dome-shaped squirrel baffle. Starlings are uncomfortable feeding under a dome and hanging on to a feeder for any length of time.

To feed American goldfinches, I use a large cheesecloth bag and fill it with thistle seed. I hang it from a wire fence in my backyard and watch the finches flock to it.
—*Marguerite Debnam*
Greensboro, North Carolina

Just because I live in an apartment doesn't mean I can't feed birds. I just hang window feeders from my picture windows. They're usually clear plastic and hang from suction cups. Most gardening centers have a variety of these handy little feeders. —*Lisa Scott*
Bloomington, Indiana

I created a safe haven below my post-mounted bird feeder for ground-feeding birds, like mourning doves, using a child's plastic swimming pool. I cut a hole in the center of the pool so I could slip it over the feeder post. Now when the doves eat the fallen seed, the neighboring cats can't see them. —*Peggy Leonard*
Fort Worth, Texas

I divided my yard into two separate feeding areas. On one side of the house, I offer finch mix, thistle (niger) and black-oil sunflower seeds. At the opposite end of the yard, I offer mixed grain and sunflower seeds. This keeps the larger birds and sparrows in one area, allowing me to enjoy an abundance of finches in the other! —*Jill Hersch*
Ayr, North Dakota

Orioles adore grape jelly, so in spring I supply it in large quantities. My oriole feeder (below) has a protective roof and a deep plastic dish, recycled from store-bought suet, for holding a heaping serving

of jelly. After the orioles leave for the South, I replace the jelly with suet for the other birds to enjoy all winter. —*Roland Jordahl*
Pelican Rapids, Minnesota

My husband suspended a muffin tin from wires to make an oriole feeder. The lip of the tin serves as a perch, and the cups hold orange halves and sugar water, which they love. —*Marcy Cella L'Anse, Michigan*

Recycle the mesh bags that oranges and other produce come in to create quick and easy bird feeders.

Fill the bags with cracked-wheat bread heels, leftover pancakes, biscuits or corn bread. Then twist the top, hang it over a clothesline or branch and secure it with a twist-tie.

A variety of birds flock to these makeshift feeders, including dark-eyed juncos that quickly gobble up the crumbs that fall to the ground. —*Henrietta Woodburn Parnell, Missouri*

When we've finished a roll of paper towel, I cover the remaining tube with peanut butter and roll it in birdseed. This makes the perfect treat during any season. —*Sharon Bohdan Greenfield, Wisconsin*

Metal shower hooks work great for hanging feeders. I just snap open the hooks to remove my feeders for refilling or cleaning. They even fit over small tree branches. —*Lorraine Noerenberg Backus, Minnesota*

Filling seed feeders with small openings can be frustrating. But I found a spill-proof way to fill my feeder.

Clean and dry an empty gallon

milk or laundry detergent jug. Then remove the bottom. (Be careful! Start by cutting diagonally from corner to corner.) Leave the cover on the jug and use it as a seed scoop.

For those hard-to-fill feeders, hold it over the opening on the feeder and remove the cover. It turns into a funnel. No messy spills! —*Mabel Forbes, Sebring, Florida*

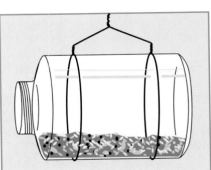

An all-weather feeder can be made from a 1-gallon glass or clear plastic jar and some wire. Simply wrap wire around the jar near each end to stabilize it and connect the two wires with a third piece. Then hang it from a tree and fill with seed. It's great because the birds are sheltered while they eat. And because the jar is clear, you can still watch them. —*Gladys Smith Greenleaf, Idaho*

Build mobile bird feeders by attaching wooden legs to wooden posts or thick branches (above). You can drill holes into the post or branch and fill with suet, attach wooden arms to hang feeders or build a tray feeder and mount it to the top. —*Roland Jordahl Pelican Rapids, Minnesota*

I bored large holes in a log and filled them with homemade suet. It's really easy and takes only minutes to make this "fantastic feeder".

—*Christine Jones Englewood, Colorado*

Windowsills with a few modifications are great places to feed the birds. I attached a board to my sill and stapled some greenery, such as pine boughs or grapevines. Then I served my feathered friends seed, fruit or nuts on the board.
—*Lisa Scott, Bloomington, Indiana*

Inexpensive tube feeders work quite well, but I have problems with the flimsy caps breaking. Luckily, I've discovered the lids to peanut butter jars are the same size. They're brighter and last much longer.
—*Will Griffin, Vestaburg, Michigan*

An old-fashioned pulley wash line runs from our porch to a tree across the yard. Our feeders and a hanging water dish are strung from the line. When it comes time to fill them, we just reel them in.

—*Maryan Daily Dallas, Pennsylvania*

Woodpeckers seem to prefer wooden feeders because they're much easier for them to grip.
—*Glen Jones, Decatur, Georgia*

By George... The best way to attract cardinals to your yard is with a tray feeder that offers flat perching surfaces (below). To protect the birds from predators, locate the feeder in or near some shrubs or other types of cover that are 3 to 6 feet high. Fill the feeder with safflower or sunflower seeds in the shell.

—*George Harrison Contributing Editor*

David Kearny

Old barbwire makes a great wreath, which doubles as a bird feeder! Just wire or tie sunflower heads to the wreath and add a cornhusk bow for good looks.

Be sure to hang the wreath where you can see it from inside the house.
—*Dick and Doni Cripe*
Chippewa Falls, Wisconsin

I make this bird-feeder kit to give to my friends and family. Inside a gift bag, place one gutter nail and a dried giant sunflower head. The gift recipient simply uses the long nail to attach the sunflower head to a wooden post. It makes a terrific bird feeder and an even better gift.
—*Allen Lyons*
Harrodsburg, Kentucky

Even with a limited budget, you can attract birds to your yard. I use the lids from large popcorn tins as feeders, punch a few holes in the sides to attach strings and a few extra holes in the bottom for drainage. I hang them from the trees outside my kitchen window.
—*Annetta Alphonso*
Port Bolivar, Texas

Sometimes the wind blows seed out of our bird feeders. So I made this 3-foot-square feeding station

IT'S A FACT...
Orioles and tanagers like raisins, currants, sugar water and sliced apples, oranges and bananas.

with a slatted side that faces the prevailing wind to block gusts (below). I can hang four feeders from it and fill the bottom as a tray feeder.
—*Mark Thomas*
Nevada City, California

When winter rolls around, there's no need to keep our children's swings up. So we take them down and hang bird feeders from the hardware.
—*Jean Fancher*
Fairmont, West Virginia

Don't throw away holiday wreaths. Instead, decorate them with treats for the birds. Attach fruit halves, peanut-butter pinecones rolled in birdseed and chunks of suet. Then hang them from a tree or shepherd's hooks. The birds love 'em.
—*Diane Johnson*
Hutchinson, Minnesota

Chisel out the centers of tree stumps and fill them with nuts and seeds for ground-feeding birds and critters. *—Annette MacDonald Hampton, Ontario*

After birds have eaten all the seeds from our sunflower heads, I use the empty heads to serve up another treat.

I boil 1-1/2 cups of water and add enough cornmeal so that it cooks into a soft mush. Removing the mixture from the heat, I add 1/2 cup of peanut butter and as much birdseed as I can before the mix becomes too stiff.

After its cools, I press the mixture into the empty sunflower heads and place them among the branches of our crab apple tree.

—Martha McDonald Carleton, Michigan

I use a standard wire cooling rack for baking to attract birds. Simply hang the rack from a feeder (any direction will do) and insert peanuts between the wires. The blue jays love it, as you can see in this photo (below)! *—R. Puterbaugh Dayton, Ohio*

Woodpecker peanut feeders are a great way to attract lots of birds, including nuthatches (above). It seems many birds enjoy picking at the nuts through the wire mesh.

—Stacy Dorsett, Macomb, Illinois

Provide corn for your feathered friends by tying a wire basket (like the ones used for gathering eggs) to a tree branch. Place several dried corncobs into the basket. The birds can easily pick off kernels.

—Jason Albrecht Milverton, Ontario

Here's how to make an inexpensive suet feeder that can't be used by starlings, blue jays or other pesky birds: After mixing the suet ingredients, roll the mixture into balls slightly smaller than the circumference of a plastic cup. Once they've set, place a suet ball in the cup, enclose the cup in a mesh produce bag, flip it upside down and hang it outside. The pesky birds can't figure out how to dangle upside down to reach the suet, but others can.

—Larry and Pat Hunter San Pierre, Indiana

I improved the standard milk-jug feeder. Instead of cutting a circle into the carton, I cut a U-shape into the side. Then fold the plastic flap inside and back out again. I'll cut off all but 1/2 inch of the flap, which serves as an awning to protect the seed from the elements.

—*Keith Pardue, Almo, Kentucky*

For a feeder with a view, cut a hollow dried gourd in half (from top to bottom) and make a half-circle opening, centered in the widest part of the gourd. Then position the gourd on a piece of Plexiglas that's about the same size as the gourd half. Adhere the gourd to the Plexiglas with all-weather adhesive. Hang the gourd from a suction cup on a picture window so you can watch from inside as the birds dine.

You can also use this method to make observation birdhouses. Just cut the proper-size entrance hole in the gourd instead of the larger half-circle opening. (See page 18 for recommended entrance hole sizes.)

—*Michael Taylor*
Lewisport, Kentucky

When my family purchased a new electric stove, I wanted to find ways to use the old one. So I took the broiler pan and converted it into a tray feeder. It drains well and is easy for cardinals, titmice, blue jays and squirrels to feed from.

—*Phyllis Shaffer, Brazil, Indiana*

We hang a bird feeder from the eaves over our second-story window so we can open the window to refill it. To provide cover from predators and a place for birds to perch, we attach evergreen boughs to the feeder.

—*Joanne Lynk*
Wadena,
Minnesota

Flickers don't like landing on a flat surface to eat. So I designed a "flicker board" to accommodate them.

I cut a 1- x 4-inch board the length of my feeder and attached it to the base. Then I nailed 3/4-inch x 1/4-inch wood strips vertically to the board, creating "rungs" similar to a ladder. The birds cling to the strips rather than balancing on the side of the feeder. Other birds, like blue jays, also use this contraption.

—*Richard Graham, Paris, Michigan*

By George... Birds really don't care if you spend $30 for a redwood barn feeder or if you scrounge something from the attic or the woods. The attractiveness of a bird feeder satisfies people more than birds.
—*George Harrison*
Contributing Editor

Use pint-size plastic strawberry containers (available at your local grocery store) as suet baskets. Simply create an enclosed container by connecting the two baskets with twist-ties. They're easy to hang from the branches of trees.
—*Cathlyn Ramsey, Wichita, Kansas*

My thistle feeder was anything *but* a fantastic feeder…until I wired an old hubcap to the bottom of it (pictured below). Now, all the spilled seed is caught, giving birds another spot to dine. —*Deck Hunter Big Horn, Wyoming*

I made an effective tray feeder by attaching a round pan from an old steamer to a post. It drains quickly, plus it's easy to tell when it needs refilling. I placed a PVC pipe around the feeder's post to keep the squirrels off of it.

You can use any kind of pan or

> **IT'S A FACT…**
> Most birds that use post-mounted or hanging feeders prefer black-oil sunflower seeds.

tray. Just drill small holes in the bottom. —*June Wescott Brewster, Nebraska*

My dad made a clever and effective feeder from a coconut shell. He cut it in half and baked it upside down for several hours on low heat. Then he drilled three holes spaced evenly around the edge of each half and attached them together with wire, leaving about an inch of space between them.

The birdseed in the coconut stays dry this way, and only the small birds can get at it. Plus, it withstands the weather nicely. —*Sue Horsley Las Vegas, Nevada*

Remove the cap from a 1/2-gallon or gallon milk jug. Then cut a 2-inch circle into the side of the jug. Fill the container with birdseed, stopping at the bottom of the hole. Birds of any size and even flying squirrels will eat from this simple feeder (see page 19 for photo proof).
—*Pauline Yeaton Farmington, Maine*

When the plants in my hanging baskets die, I spread a little wild birdseed on the potting soil. It germinates, and the birds are left with some safe green spaces many feet above the dangers of the lawn.
—*C. Hartzell, Manassas, Virginia*

Use different-size plastic soda bottles as thistle (niger) feeders. Cut four 1/4-inch feeding slits into the sides of the bottle and four corresponding holes a few inches below them to insert small wooden dowels for perches. It's a "cheep" way to feed the finches.

—*Matthew Yoder*
Bloomfield, Iowa

←1/4" slit

When the bluebirds

come to nest in our backyard, we provide them with an easy meal. We hang a flat tray feeder a few feet from the nesting box and place mealworms on it. The male bluebird often grabs some food for the female, and once the eggs hatch, the parents can quickly find food for their hungry young.

—*Brenda Bevilacqua*
Charlottesville, Virginia

Steller's jays were devouring my suet. So I attached a basic wire suet cage to a flat board that's 2 to 3 inches larger than the feeder on each side. Then I hung the board so that the feeder is below it. Only downy woodpeckers and nuthatches could get to it. When I hung the board at a slight angle, I attracted more woodpeckers, but the jays still couldn't

find a way to hang onto the feeder.

I've also placed a wooden peaked roof over another suet cage. Woodpeckers, orioles, nuthatches and black-headed grosbeaks have little problem using this one. The jays also manage to get a little suet from this feeder, but it's entertaining to watch their awkward attempts.

—*Kay Williams*
Placerville, California

I have a flowerpot post that several potted plants hang from in summer (pictured above, at left). In winter, I remove the pots and place a bird feeder on top of the post (above right). Now it serves me year-round.

—*Adelaide Kearney*
West Mifflin, Pennsylvania

***By George*...**Far more practical and less expensive than buying bird food is planting food-bearing trees, shrubs and plants in your backyard. (For ideas, turn to "Perfect Plantings", which starts on page 79. —*George Harrison*
Contributing Editor

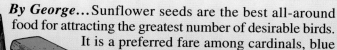

By George... Sunflower seeds are the best all-around food for attracting the greatest number of desirable birds. It is a preferred fare among cardinals, blue jays, chickadees, finches, grosbeaks, titmice, nuthatches and crossbills.
—*George Harrison, Contributing Editor*

I removed the swings and other apparatus from my children's unused swing set and turned it into a feeding station. There are plenty of hooks to hang a variety of feeders.
—*Mrs. Jonathon Zehr*
Milverton, Ontario

Gay Bumgarner

American goldfinches (above) camp out in my yard year-round since I planted sunflowers. They strip the plants of nearly all their leaves, but the plants continue to thrive. Then they, and many other seed-loving birds, eat the seeds when they ripen.   —*Mollie Haag*
Ione, California

Don't throw away your stripped ears of corn. After the squirrels and blue jays devour the kernels, use the cob for a simple feeder. Spread some peanut butter on it, then roll it in birdseed. I put the cob back on the squirrel feeder and watch as both birds and squirrels enjoy the treat.
—*Barbara Bailie*
Jefferson City, Missouri

We hang our hummingbird feeders below the eaves of our house. I used to need a ladder to take them down each time I filled them. Now, I simply make feeder hooks from coat hangers and use a long piece of PVC plumbing pipe to raise and lower the feeders.   —*Diane Golly*
Rocklin, California

The soil in our backyard is so hard it's nearly impossible to dig a hole. When we bought a pole for our bird feeder, my husband, David, came up with a clever idea. He used a wide-based Christmas tree stand to hold it upright. Now the feeder can be moved anywhere in our yard.
—*Lurane Slaght, Tucson, Arizona*

IT'S A FACT...
Most birds have an undeveloped sense of smell and locate their food by sight.

Chapter 3
Setting the Table

*W*hen it comes to picky eaters, many birds are like children. The food must be familiar and offered on the proper "plate".

For instance, finches like their seed in tube feeders (at left), while northern cardinals prefer platforms. Dark-eyed juncos and mourning doves would rather scratch around at ground level.

So when you set up a bird cafeteria in your backyard, keep in mind that the more variety you offer, the greater variety of customers you'll attract.

This chapter is packed with reader tips that are sure to make your yard the most popular buffet in the neighborhood. In fact, you may be surprised to see how many feathered friends will line up for dinner at your place.

Photo: Richard Day/Daybreak Imagery

I place fruit slices in my suet basket. The woodpeckers enjoy the special snack. —*Richele Herigan Harrisburg, Pennsylvania*

Offer pea-size pieces of cat food, stale nuts and dried fruits on a flat surface. Birds, especially blue jays, flock to this treat. —*Tina Jacobs Wantage, New Jersey*

My dogs don't always eat all of their dry dog food, so we offer the leftovers to the birds. We attract several varieties of wild birds to it. —*Linda McCullough-Fuhrman West Palm Beach, Florida*

I've discovered that orioles prefer the cheaper generic brands of grape jelly to the more expensive name brands. —*Colleen Johnson Monticello, Minnesota*

To save money, we put inexpensive chicken scratch in our large bird feeders and regular birdseed in the smaller ones. The large birds don't mind eating the cheaper scratch. Even smaller birds snack on tiny pieces. —*Wyvon Dawson Webb City, Missouri*

I place a handful of peanuts on my deck whenever I see blue jays in the backyard (below). As a result, they now associate me with food and often come to the patio

Morris and Mary Oberlin

door looking for me. It's a really fun relationship for this retired person. —*Connie Coloutes, Poland, Ohio*

Offering sand or fine gravel with birdseed helps birds digest their food. We have a small children's

---

I finally came up with a way to hang my bird feeders high enough so that my neighbors' cats can't reach them.

A wire coat hanger offers the perfect solution. I simply straighten the hanger, then bend it so it has a hook on each end and a loop in the middle.

I use one hook to hold the feeder. Then I lift it by the loop, using a long stick with a nail in one end (see illustration at right). I hook the other end on a branch high in my backyard trees, well out of the cats' reach. —*Charles Allen Bellingham, Washington*

Scatter raisins around your yard immediately after spotting your first American robin in spring. Because they'll often arrive when the ground is frozen, it's hard for them to find worms. So they really make use of this offering. They'll even continue to snack on the raisins after the ground thaws.

—*Ruth Woltring*
Grafton, Wisconsin

sandbox in our yard where birds get this grit, but we also provide a dish of it alongside the seed.

—*James Thiessen*
Hodgson, Manitoba

The Granny Smith apple tree in our yard is a favorite place for the birds. So we leave some of the fruit on the tree for them. When all the leaves fall in autumn, we have a perfect view of our feathered friends snacking on the tart apples.

—*Marjorie Henry*
Portland, Oregon

Pop a bag of microwave popcorn to give the birds an extra special treat. Sprinkle it on the ground and put some in a tray feeder. And don't forget to save a small bowl for yourself.

—*Colette Pierce*
Miniota, Manitoba

Instead of buying expensive bags of corn to feed the birds and

squirrels, I ask a local farmer if I can walk through his cornfield after he harvests it. You'll be surprised how many ears fall to the ground during the picking process.

—*Shirley Henry, Newark, New York*

We buy unsalted peanuts and "hide" them underneath the bark of our trees. (Trees with shaggy bark work best.) Blue jays, nuthatches, chickadees, tufted titmice (above), flickers, woodpeckers and other birds hunt for the peanuts throughout our yard. It's almost become a game between the birds and us.

—*Mike Fallon, Straughn, Indiana*

Most jam and jelly recipes using fruit pectin advise cooks to skim off the foam and discard it before canning.

Since I put grape jelly in my suet mixture, I decided to save the "skimmings" and use them instead. It works great—the birds love it!
— *Mary Lewis, Satanta, Kansas*

Bake sunflower seeds in the oven for 20 minutes at 250° before filling your feeders. This will keep the ones that fall to the ground from sprouting. — *Margie Price Broken Arrow, Oklahoma*

Salt bricks aren't just for deer, squirrels and rabbits. Much to my surprise, I've seen birds—especially purple finches—enjoying them too. — *Esther Dunkelberger Mifflintown, Pennsylvania*

To ensure my backyard birds receive enough calcium, I add crushed eggshells to their seed. To do this, thoroughly rinse a few eggshells, put them on a cookie sheet and bake at 350° until they're dry. Use a rolling pin or spoon to crush them into fine pieces and mix into your birdseed or suet. — *Tonja Karnes Hopkins, Michigan*

Peel one side of an apple, score it a little bit and hang it from a tree branch with wire. The finches really love this summer treat. Even butterflies stop by to feed on the juice. — *Lu Reed, Spencer, Iowa*

Seed stays dry in our modified tray feeder (right). We drilled a hole and placed a 1-foot bolt through the bottom of the tray so the threaded end faced up. Then we held it in place by tightening a washer and nut.

We threaded another nut and washer about 3/4 inch from the top of the bolt and placed a recycled aluminum light shade onto it. Then we held it tight with another washer and nut.
— *Susan Benjamin Baton Rouge, Louisiana*

If your home is made of brick, spread a mix of peanut butter, cornmeal and birdseed into the mortar joints. Woodpeckers love it, especially in winter. It's also a good mixture to spread onto the bark of trees.
— *Lisa Scott, Bloomington, Indiana*

I purchase bulk quantities of beef kidney fat (true suet) at a local meat packing plant. Then I divide and wrap them into 1- to 2-pound portions, just enough to fill my wire suet basket. I'll freeze the sealed packages until a refill is needed. Woodpeckers, chickadees, tufted titmice, blue jays, nuthatches and Carolina wrens love snacking on it.
— *Burton Tiffany Aiken, South Carolina*

When I make peanut butter and jelly sandwiches, I make an extra one for the birds and slip it into a suet basket. The woodpeckers devour them.

I also take the leftover heels from bread and hold them together with peanut butter. Then I coat the outside with some more peanut butter and place them in my square suet cage.
—*Tina Jacobs*
Wantage, New Jersey

Pine nuts are a real treat that chickadees and nuthatches love. These nuts, which are often used in ethnic dishes, are good for the birds because they're high in fat, so it keeps the birds energized through cold winter nights.
—*Duncan Campbell*
Fredericton, New Brunswick

I invite more birds to my backyard feeders by providing several nearby perches I call "staging areas". Birds use these perches—made from dead tree branches—as checkpoints to make sure everything is safe as they approach a feeder.

Not only do these additional perches bring more songbirds to my backyard, they also help my feathered friends keep an eye out for predators.
—*Janet Lenz*
DeSoto, Missouri

Catbirds (above) are one of my favorite backyard visitors. So it was a welcome surprise when I discovered they relish the grape jelly that I put out for orioles.

Although they're known as shy birds, they became friendlier as they continued to feed on the jelly throughout summer. After awhile, they even kept eating as I was gardening nearby.
—*Paula Smits*
DePere, Wisconsin

ASK GEORGE

How can I discourage ground-feeding birds, such as mourning doves, from using my platform feeder? My feeder is mounted 7 feet high on a post.
—*Walter Mullaney*
Arden, North Carolina

George: Try mounting a roof about 3 inches above the platform. This should exclude doves from feeding, but still allow enough room for smaller birds to use the feeder.

To attract American goldfinches and dark-eyed juncos, I make several bouquets of dried-up flowers and hang them from tree branches. Sunflowers, coneflowers, black-eyed Susans and other flowers that produce lots of seeds are perfect for these bouquets. —*Marla Bench Vancouver, Washington*

Peggy Bruce

I've experimented with a wild birdseed blend that included dried cherries. Soon after, I noticed eastern bluebirds (above) stopping at our feeder. Bluebirds don't normally eat seeds, so I grabbed my binoculars to get a better look. The birds were plucking the dried cherries from the mixture. Now I always throw a couple handfuls of dried cherries or raisins into the seed when I refill the feeder.
—*Mrs. Dallas Walker Milan, Georgia*

I keep a supply of bird food in my car. I'll mix old cereal, leftover holiday nuts and other energy-rich foods. Then when I stop at the park or go hiking, I'll sprinkle it on the ground for the local winged residents. —*Gloria Douglas Palm Bay, Florida*

IT'S A FACT... About one-third of all American adults feed wild birds in their backyard.

Feed birds at the same time every day. They'll get to know your routine and greet you as you fill the feeders. —*Robert Kaufman McClure, Illinois*

Collect the crumbs from the bottom of cereal boxes in a resealable plastic bag. When you have a cup or more, add them to your favorite suet recipe. It's a great way to get rid of these little extras that clutter up the pantry. —*Carolyn Hylton Covington, Virginia*

Squirrels ruined our finches' favorite thistle feeder. So my husband and I came up with a solution. I spread a thin layer of peanut butter on an empty toilet paper roll and rolled it in thistle seed (right). Then my husband created a metal "T" and welded a metal  washer to the bottom. The seed-covered tube slips over the washer and rests on the cross of the T. It hangs upside down from the washer on a pole the squirrels can't climb.
—*Rebecca King Burlison, Tennessee*

Carolina wrens actually ate bird-seed when we added dried bacon bits to the mixture.

—*Dot and David Hinman*
Blairsville, Georgia

Mealworms are bluebirds' favorite treat, so I make sure they've always got a good supply. To grow your own mealworms, begin with a 5-gallon plastic bucket and add a mixture of hay and dirt so it's about half full. Now add a dozen or so mealworms. Sprinkle the contents with water and provide a little ground steer feed two to three times a week. (Cornmeal also works—see alternative method on page 180.) Place a screen over the bucket to keep the worms confined.

—*Anna Chupp*
Shipshewana, Indiana

Fill your feeders using old juice pitchers—you won't spill a single seed. And if the pitchers have covers, they make good storage containers as well. —*Debbie Smith*
Cabot, Pennsylvania

By George... If a backyard offers nothing but food, it may attract a limited number of birds on a fairly regular basis, but the combination of food and cover is better.

—*George Harrison*
Contributing
Editor

Pecans are a favorite of the birds in my yard. Since they're expensive, I wait until mine have lost their fresh taste. Then I put a handful of the nuts in a mesh bag and hang it from a tree limb. It doesn't take long for the birds to find this treat.

—*Mary Westmoreland*
Snyder, Texas

My Cyclone fence helps me attract birds. Every morning, I slice a few apples and an orange. Then I spear the fruit onto the top of the chain-link fence. Blue jays, northern cardinals, northern mockingbirds and woodpeckers arrive to feast.

—*David Dunn*
Baton Rouge, Louisiana

Hollow out your pumpkins and fill them with cracked corn and birdseed to give ground-feeding birds a special autumn treat. The doves seem to really enjoy corn. I like to call it my "twick or tweet".

—*Gloria Meredith*
Harrington, Delaware

Deer hunting is a popular outdoor activity where I live. Instead of discarding deer fat, I store it in resealable plastic bags and freeze it. Then in winter, I place it in a suet basket for my feathered friends.

—*Elaine Morrison*
Deloraine, Manitoba

I make a festive Christmas treat for backyard birds (right). I begin with a 1/2-inch dowel that's 24 inches long. Then I cut three pieces from a 1-inch x 4-inch cedar board. One measures 14 inches long and the other two are 10 and 7 inches long.

Drill a 1/2-inch hole in the center of each board and position them several inches apart on the dowel. Then secure the dowel in an 8-inch flowerpot filled with plaster of Paris. Spread your favorite suet recipe on the tree's three levels, and set it out for the birds to enjoy.
—*Jeanne Price*
Naples, Florida

Downy woodpeckers (above) and other birds can't resist peanut butter-dipped pinecones. During the holiday season, I attach a festive red ribbon to the pinecones and hang them from my trees.
—*Roland Jordahl*
Pelican Rapids, Minnesota

A coconut is an extra special treat for the birds. Simply split the coconut in half, drill three evenly spaced holes around the rim and hang it. We fill ours with seed and bacon grease, too. —*Elaine Wade*
Jackson, Michigan

When I ran out of suet, I began thinking creatively and put together these easy-to-make treats. I toasted two slices of bread, covered both sides of each slice with peanut butter and pressed them in birdseed. The two slices fit nicely into my suet basket, and the birds seem to love them! —*Sarah Self*
Birmingham, Alabama

When using egg whites, don't throw away the yolks. Scramble them (don't add any ingredients), cool and put them on your bird feeder. —*Nancy Spear*
Gilford, New Hampshire

My kids like to help feed our backyard birds, but they can't reach the feeder. So I showed them how to make feeders of their own.

We spread peanut butter on the outside of plastic cups and roll them in a pan of birdseed. Then we poke a hole in the bottom of the cups, attach a ribbon and hang them like bells from a tree right outside our living room window. The kids love watching birds eat from their home-made feeders. —*Kay Waldvogel Osakis, Minnesota*

When cobs of sweet corn become too ripe to eat, I place them on my tray feeder. The birds love feasting on the kernels. —*Gary Clark Knowlton, Quebec*

Provide birds with a wealth of food by planting a vegetable garden. The robins love the earthworms the fertile ground yields. And insect-eating birds, such as bluebirds, swallows, catbirds and cowbirds, protect the crops. Cedar waxwings will visit the strawberries. House finches

and American goldfinches will feast on lettuce that's gone to seed. Hummingbirds love my patch of jewelweed. If you're lucky, the birds will save some of the produce for you! —*Dorothy Dickerson Albion, Michigan*

Billie Silvey

Since I placed a suet feeder near my bluebird house (like the one above), lovely eastern varieties have been attracted to both the food and the nest box each spring.

—*David Kent, Richmond, Virginia*

ASK GEORGE

How can we stop birds from spilling the seed in our thistle feeder? —*Elaine McCoy Xenia, Ohio*

George: If seeds are being spilled, the feeder is faulty or the feeding ports are too large to contain the tiny niger (thistle) seed, which only works in feeders with small ports.

Also, consider that when birds eat niger, they crack the seed, eat the heart and discard the shells. Look closely to see if you're mistaking these tiny empty hulls for spilled uneaten seed. From a distance, they look alike.

A cored apple filled with peanut butter makes a fantastic bird treat. Run yarn or heavy string through the apple or set it on a tray feeder. The fruit has been a big hit—especially when the weather gets really cold.
—*Melissa Vice, Milford, Ohio*

After I found a box of outdated fruit-filled cereal bars, I decided to offer them to the birds. They gobbled them up. The next morning, I over-browned a strudel bar in the toaster and placed it on my feeder. They loved that, too. —*Gwen Hall Marietta, Georgia*

Birds really enjoy hickory nuts. All you have to do is find a way to break their rock-hard shells.

I hold them with pliers, hit them with a hammer (wear safety goggles for protection) and place the broken nuts—shells and all—in my

Basement Inventor Shares Feeder Filler

MANY of the peanut butter suet recipes I've tried attract tons of birds to our suet log, but they're a mess to handle. So my wife and I developed an easy-to-use suet pump that leaves us with clean hands after each refill.

It took some poking around at the hardware store, but with the help of a knowledgeable clerk, we came up with this effective design made from white 1-1/2-inch PVC plumbing pipe and gray PVC electrical conduit (the conduit nests nicely into the white pipe).

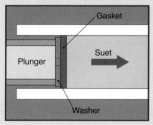

Use epoxy to attach an extra large "fender washer" onto one end of the gray conduit (be sure to center it). Then cut a rubber gasket slightly larger than the washer so it fits snuggly into the white pipe. Center and glue the gasket onto the washer.

To use the pump, fill most of the white pipe with your suet mix. Then insert the plunger and hold the open end against your feeder. Push the plunger to fill the empty cavities.

We've even made refillable plugs for our feeders by using the pump to press out round tube-like strips of suet. Then we cut them just long enough to fill the bird feeder's holes and freeze them. The refills work like a charm. —*Clive and Jean Veri, Holiday Island, Arkansas*

bird feeders. The birds pick out the meats and carry away the pieces.

—*Kenneth Searfoss*
Reading, Pennsylvania

I filled lime halves that I used for baking with a mixture of peanut butter and birdseed. To my surprise, the birds devoured them. I've served the mixture in lemon and orange halves as well, and I often add citrus to my homemade suet.

—*Lin Edmonds*
Winston-Salem, North Carolina

I make small bird feeders from orange halves. Just scoop out the pulp, poke three evenly spaced holes around edge and tie strings to the holes. Knot the ends together at the top so you can hang them from a branch. Then fill them with peanut butter, bread crumbs, nuts and birdseed. —*Gloria Meredith*
Harrington, Delaware

The most successful seed mix in my backyard is made of:
- 40% black-oil sunflower seeds
- 25% striped sunflower seeds
- 10% sunflower hearts
- 10% millet
- 10% corn
- 5% safflower seeds

—*Robert Carlson, Davenport, Iowa*

IT'S A FACT...
Discourage blackbirds from raiding your feeder by eliminating seed mix that includes cracked corn.

Jack Jones

My puppy refused to eat the new dog food I bought, so I offered it to the birds at my feeder. It wasn't long before a red-headed woodpecker (above) showed up to carry away most of the food.

—*Murry MacDonald*
Wilmington, North Carolina

I began adding 1/4 pound of ground beef to my feeder every morning. Now the birds practically wait for me to fill it up. I get daily visits from northern cardinals, sparrows, woodpeckers and northern mockingbirds. —*Bud Schmidt*
Tucson, Arizona

Add a cup of sand to the birdseed in your feeder. The gritty granules help birds digest food. I just leave the bag of sand alongside my stored seed. —*Earlene Maness*
Des Moines, Iowa

During the holidays, I bake extra gingerbread cookies to leave on my platform feeders. The squirrels also enjoy snacking on these treats.
—*Leslie Demargerie
Sprague, Manitoba*

Birdseed can go stale if it's not stored in an airtight container. I also buy fresh seed in smaller quantities, so I can use it before it goes bad. —*Tom Kovach
Park Rapids, Minnesota*

When worms are scarce in early spring, I leave pieces of suet on the ground for the American robins. They feed on it until the weather warms. —*Phyllis Schabacker
Fountain City, Wisconsin*

Looking for a way to keep your bulk birdseed safe from furry critters? Try using an old metal cooler, like I do.

I purchased this one (above) at a flea market, and it's worked like a charm. It holds quite a bit of seed and keeps it fresh as well
—*Paul Hondorp
Byron Center, Michigan*

Bluebirds love cooked grits. In fact, that's how we enticed a pair to nest in our backyard—we left a batch out every morning prior to nesting season. —*Charlotte Heinze
Davie, Florida*

ASK GEORGE

Microwaving birdseed is a great way to keep it from sprouting in my lawn, but I'm worried it has a negative effect on the seeds' nutritional value. What's your opinion?
—*Barbara Chidester, Homedale, Idaho*

George: Microwaves do not affect the nutritional value of human foods, so there's no reason to believe they would reduce the nutrition of birdseed.

To stop stray sprouts without a microwave, use niger seed (thistle), which already has been sterilized. Others, like sunflower seed in the shell, may grow a few sprouts but shouldn't be a huge problem.

IT'S A FACT...
Clean bird feeders regularly—nobody likes to eat off of dirty dishes.

To keep my birdseed from going bad, I store it in empty plastic ice cream containers and place it in the freezer. One container is enough to fill my feeders.   —*Julie Kamm*
New Ulm, Minnesota

We set out orange slices for the orioles and suet for the woodpeckers. But we received an added bonus when we realized catbirds enjoy both these bird treats, too.
—*Dave and Bonnie Downs*
Dodgeville, Wisconsin

I accidentally discovered a terrific springtime meal for young birds. I set out a few slices of raw potato, and a mother bird stopped by to feed her fledglings pieces of it.
—*Lillian Williams, Houston, Texas*

Each spring I plant a cheerful patch of sunflowers—from towering giants to dainty small ones, and a bunch of varieties in between. Come autumn, when the sunflowers reach their prime, I harvest the largest ones and leave the smaller heads for the chickadees, nuthatches and finches to feed on.

I'll hang the large heads in my basement to dry. When the seeds begin falling from them, I'll pluck the rest of the seeds and store them in an airtight container until winter.
—*Justime Morris, Revenna, Ohio*

Gail Varney

Many people feed grape jelly and oranges to birds like Baltimore orioles (that's a female above). But I've also discovered strawberry preserves are a great way to attract these birds. I smear it on toast, sometimes serving it with peanut butter as well. They love it!
—*Donna Jablonski*
Kulpmont, Pennsylvania

By George...There are at least four feeding niches to be filled at any feeding station—ground level, table-top (post), hanging and tree trunk.
—*George Harrison*
Contributing
Editor

53

Birds and Their Favorite Foods

	Niger (thistle) seed	Cracked corn	White proso millet	Black-oil sunflower seed	Hulled sunflower seed	Beef suet	Fruit	*Sugar water/ nectar
Rose-breasted grosbeak				●	●			
Black-headed grosbeak				●	●			
Evening grosbeak		●	●	●	●			
Northern cardinal		●	●	●	●		●	
Indigo bunting	●				●			
Eastern towhee	●	●	●	●	●			
Dark-eyed junco	●	●	●	●	●			
White-crowned sparrow	●	●	●	●	●			
White-throated sparrow	●	●	●	●	●			
American tree sparrow	●	●	●		●			
Chipping sparrow	●	●	●		●			
Song sparrow	●	●	●		●			
House sparrow	●	●	●	●	●			
House finch	●	●	●	●	●			
Purple finch	●	●	●	●	●			
American goldfinch	●	●	●	●	●			
Pine siskin	●	●	●	●	●			
Scarlet tanager							●	●
Western tanager							●	●
Baltimore oriole							●	●
Red-winged blackbird		●		●	●			
Eastern bluebird							●	
Wood thrush							●	
American robin							●	
Gray catbird							●	
Northern mockingbird							●	
Brown thrasher							●	
Ruby-throated hummingbird								●
Anna's hummingbird								●
Broad-tailed hummingbird								●
Tufted titmouse	●			●	●	●		
Black-capped chickadee	●			●	●	●		
White-breasted nuthatch				●	●	●		
Carolina wren						●		
Cedar waxwing							●	
Woodpecker				●	●	●	●	
Scrub jay		●		●	●	●	●	
Blue jay		●		●	●	●	●	
Mourning dove	●	●	●		●			
Northern bobwhite		●	●					
Ring-necked pheasant		●	●		●			
Canada goose		●						
Mallard		●						

* To make sugar water for hummingbirds, mix 4 parts water with 1 part sugar. Boil, cool and serve. Store leftovers in the refrigerator for up to a week. Change feeder nectar every 3 to 5 days.

Source: *Garden Birds of America* by George H. Harrison. Willow Creek Press, 1996.

Chapter 4
Award-Winning Recipes

Company's coming—of the feathered variety, that is.

To keep your dinner guests satisfied, try some of these special recipes sent in by readers from across North America.

You may be surprised. Many of them use ingredients you probably already have in the pantry.

And once you spice up the offerings, you're likely to see more winged activity in your backyard than ever before.

So even though it means a little extra time in the kitchen, expanding the menu for your feathered friends will keep them comin' back for seconds…and thirds.

Photo: F.C. and Janice Bergquist

My homemade bird feed attracts woodpeckers, eastern bluebirds and northern cardinals (to prove it, I took the photo below). It's easy to make. I just whip up a *big* batch, then freeze the leftovers until needed.

Start by mixing 10 pounds of yellow cornmeal with 5 pounds of flour. Then melt 7 cups of lard and 3 cups of peanut butter. Pour the liquid mixture gradually over the dry

ingredients, blending until it reaches a fairly firm consistency. Add raisins, cracked peanuts and—in early spring—crushed eggshells, too.

Roll the mix into a "log" or press it in a pan. Place the mixture in the freezer until it's firm enough to cut to fit your feeder (I use a pizza cutter). Freeze extras in plastic bags until you're ready to serve them.

—*Gary Chandler*
McKenzie, Tennessee

Northern mockingbirds aren't the only birds that love my "Mockingbird Muffins". They're a hit with many feathered friends.

> *1 cup cornmeal*
> *1 cup flour*
> *1 cup grated bread crumbs*
> *1/2 tablespoon baking soda*
> *3/4 cup currants or raisins*
> *1/2 cup bacon drippings*
> *1/4 teaspoon sand*
> *1 cup water*

Combine cornmeal, flour, bread crumbs and baking soda in a medium bowl. Add currants or raisins, bacon drippings, sand and water. Mix well. Spoon into muffin cups. Bake at 350° for 15 minutes. Serve on a tray feeder or spear onto tree branches. —*Mildred Unruh*
Ambler, Pennsylvania

Here's a simple backyard bird treat that can be made with basic ingredients most people already have in the house.

> *1 cup peanut butter*
> *1 cup oats*
> *1 cup corn muffin mix*
> *1 cup canned corn*
> *1 cup raisins*
> *1 cup birdseed*
> *Chopped apple or grapes, optional*

In a bowl, mix all the ingredients. The consistency should be thicker than cookie dough. Mold the treat into squares, then fill your suet feeder. Wrap the rest in plastic and store in the freezer.

When I serve these treats, the birds devour them in a matter of hours! —*Margaret Widger*
Philadelphia, Pennsylvania

I make this fruity suet for my feathered friends. Mix melted lard with chopped oranges, raisins, seeds and peanuts. Pour into tuna or cat food cans and store in your refrigerator. The birds can't resist it, especially on cold winter days.

—*Tonja Karnes*
Hopkins, Michigan

We've been offering our feathered friends this special treat since my children were young. They used to love watching the variety of birds that flocked to it. Here's the recipe:

2 cups cooking grease
5 cups cornmeal
3 cups flour
1 cup barley
1 cup rice
2 or 3 eggs
Milk or water

Mix all the ingredients together and thin with the milk or water to the consistency of cake dough. Spread onto baking sheets and bake at 350° for 30-40 minutes. Let cool and crumble. Sprinkle the crumbs onto a tray feeder or on the ground and watch as the birds fly in to feast.

—*Ruth Wathen*
Evansville, Indiana

This nectar recipe is irresistible to hummingbirds and orioles. Prepare the basic sugar water mix (4 cups water to 1 cup sugar, boil and cool), then add in my special ingredient—a couple drops of orange extract. The birds will flock to it.

—*Anna Frie, Burtrum, Minnesota*

IT'S A FACT...
Many birds migrate because the food they eat becomes scarce during certain seasons.

Save empty sunflower heads and press this mixture onto them. The birds will thank you for it.

1 cup water
Yellow cornmeal
1/2 cup oats
1/2 cup peanut butter
Wild birdseed

Boil water and mix in just enough cornmeal to cook into a soft mixture. Remove from heat and add oats, peanut butter and birdseed. Make sure the mixture doesn't get too thick. Press into sunflower heads and hang from a tree or bird feeder.

—*Gloria Meredith*
Harrington, Delaware

Attract woodpeckers, as well as chickadees and nuthatches, with this tropical treat. The best part is this suet mix won't melt when it's warm outside.

1 cup lard
1 cup peanut butter
1/3 cup coconut
2-1/2 cups oats
2-1/2 cups cornmeal
Raisins, nuts or birdseed, optional

Melt lard and peanut butter. Stir in coconut, oats and cornmeal. Add optional ingredients. Pour the mixture into a pan and chill in refrigerator overnight. Cut into squares and wrap in plastic for easy storage.

—*Rebecca Beiler*
Lancaster, Pennsylvania

F. C. Bergquist

I've discovered a great oriole food that can be served in a sugar-water feeder (above). Simply mix 1/3 quart grape jelly with 3 cups water and blend well. The orioles can't get enough of this fruity nectar.

—*Marianne Budahn*
Darwin, Minnesota

Here's a recipe I call "Cardinal Casserole". It's a backyard bird favorite:

>   *1 cup cornmeal*
>   *1 cup rolled oats*
>   *1/2 cup bacon grease*
>   *1 cup flour*
>   *3 tablespoons dried milk*
>   *1/2 cup bread crumbs*
>   *1 cup water*
>   *1/2 teaspoon baking soda*

Combine all ingredients in order

listed and mix well. Bake in a 1-pound coffee can for 1 hour at 350°. You can also bake it in potpie tins, so the portions fit into your suet feeders.

—*Ruth Wathen*
Evansville, Indiana

Make this "Summer Heat Bird Treat" when it's above 70°:

>   *1-1/2 cups water*
>   *1 cup oats*
>   *3/4 cup bacon grease or lard, melted*
>   *1 cup uncooked Cream of Wheat*
>   *1 cup cornmeal or hominy grits*
>   *1/2 cup raisins*
>   *1-1/2 cups creamy peanut butter*
>   *2 handfuls birdseed*

Boil water and add oats. Reduce heat and simmer for 1 minute. Remove from the stove and stir in ingredients in the order listed. Let the mixture cool and place in suet feeders for immediate use. Freeze unused portions in resealable bags.

—*Anna Frie, Burtrum, Minnesota*

I've shared this bird feed recipe with all my friends, and it's received rave reviews:

>   *2 cups peanut butter*
>   *2 cups lard*
>   *1/2 cup each of flour, old-fashioned oats, Spanish peanuts, raisins, sunflower seeds and chopped corn*

Melt peanut butter and lard. Mix all ingredients in a large cake pan and refrigerate until hardened. Cut and place in suet feeders.

—*Ethel Fleming, Hemphill, Texas*

This hearty mixture attracts a large variety of birds:

1-1/2 cups wild birdseed
1 cup bread crumbs
1 cup graham cracker crumbs
1 cup melted suet
2 teaspoons sand (for grit)

Simply mix all the ingredients together and serve on a tray feeder.
—*Ann Sturgeon, Kokomo, Indiana*

All birds love this treat. If you make too much, freeze it for later!

2 cups cornmeal
6 cups water
1/2 cup bacon drippings
1 cup flour
1 rounded tablespoon sand
1/2 cup molasses
1/2 teaspoon baking powder
1 teaspoon red pepper
Nuts and raisins, optional

Mix cornmeal with water, boil and cool. Add remaining ingredients. Mix in enough additional water to bind mixture together and pack in small foil pie pans. Bake at 400° until brown. Hang the pans in a tree and watch the birds flock to the treat.
—*Bernie Bellin, Franklin, Wisconsin*

I make "Bird Baubles" as Christmas gifts for my bird-loving friends:

3-1/2 cups oats
1 quart water

1 pound lard or suet
1 jar peanut butter (12 ounces)
3-1/2 cups cornmeal
3-1/2 cups uncooked Cream of Wheat

Cook oats in water for 2 minutes. Remove from heat and stir in lard or suet and peanut butter until melted. Add cornmeal and Cream of Wheat. Cool and shape into balls. As you're forming them, add a ribbon near the top for hanging.　—*Dianne Koebke Green Bay, Wisconsin*

Birds love my "High Energy Double-Nut Tweety Treat". Keep in mind, however, that the recipe takes about 3 hours to complete:

5 to 7 pounds raw suet
1 pound fatty bacon
2 cups raw peanuts, chopped
2 cups raisins
2 cups cornmeal
2 cups oats
1 cup peanut butter
1 cup dry dog food, crushed
1 cup sunflower hearts
1/2 cup sugar
1/2 cup cracked corn or mixed seed

Cook suet over stove until melted and fry bacon until crisp (save fat). Add crumbled bacon and fat to melted suet. Add remaining ingredients. Mix well.

Allow mixture to cool completely and cut into squares that fit your suet feeder.　—*Margie Harclerode Bedford, Pennsylvania*

IT'S A FACT... Birds have higher body temperatures than mammals and must eat proportionately more to maintain them.

Make this "Bird Cake" treat and hang it from trees or bird feeders in mesh bags:

1 cup lard
1 cup crunchy peanut butter
1/2 cup honey
2 eggs
1 cup oats
1 teaspoon baking soda
2 cups whole wheat flour

Mix all ingredients and pour into a greased 9-inch square pan. Bake at 350° for 30-40 minutes or until a toothpick inserted in the center comes out clean.

—*Mary Hochstetler*
Milford, Indiana

Because of the heat here in Oklahoma, suet can become a real mess during summer. Luckily, I've found a no-melt suet recipe that allows me to serve this treat all year long. Here's what you'll need:

2 cups quick-cooking oats
2 cups cornmeal
1 cup flour
1/2 cup sugar
1 cup lard
1 cup crunchy peanut butter

Combine the oats, cornmeal, flour and sugar in a large bowl. Melt the lard and peanut butter (I use my microwave oven) and add to the dry ingredients. Mix well.

IT'S A FACT...
Chickadees are common visitors to bird feeders, but they get about 75% of their food from the wild.

Pour the suet into a square pan about 2 inches deep, or spread it onto tree limbs. —*Virginia Barnard*
Okmulgee, Oklahoma

Make "Bird Bells" in your kitchen with this simple method. You'll need these ingredients:

2 eggs
2 tablespoons honey
Birdseed
Empty plastic dairy container
from margarine, sour cream, etc.
Yarn or string

Combine egg and honey with a fork, adding birdseed until the mixture holds its shape.

Line the dairy container with plastic wrap and poke a small hole through the bottom of the container. Pull a loop of yarn or string through the hole, leaving about two inches outside the container.

Fill the container with the seed mixture and let set for about 5 days. Remove the hardened seed from the plastic container and hang the treat from a tree branch. —*Nin Neil*
Munhall, Pennsylvania

This fatty treat is a great source of nourishment for birds during the coldest months.

2/3 cup bacon grease
1 cup birdseed
1/4 cup cornmeal
1/2 cup peanut hearts

Melt bacon grease in a heavy pan over medium heat. Pour in a mixing bowl and add remaining ingredients, stirring well after each ingredient is added. Pour mixture into a freezer-safe container and chill until hardened.

Cut portions as needed, serving in a suet feeder or on a tray feeder.

—Matthew Dorfsmith
Big Bear City, California

This high-energy recipe is perfect for birds in winter, but you can make it any time of year.

> *3 cups cornmeal*
> *3 cups flour*
> *3 cups oats*
> *1 tablespoon salt*
> *2 tablespoons sugar*
> *1 tablespoon baking powder*
> *1 egg, beaten*
> *1/2 cup peanut butter*
> *1 cup melted shortening*
> *Birdseed*

Combine all ingredients and spread the mixture on a cookie sheet. Bake at 400° for 20 minutes. Let cool and cut into pieces.

—Mary Farlow, Milton, Wisconsin

We replaced suet with my pie crust recipe. The birds adore it!

Mix 1 cup flour, 1/2 cup shortening, 1/4 teaspoon salt and just enough water to form a ball. There's no need to bake it, just put the treat out near your seed feeders and watch it disappear.

—Linda Byler
Middlefield, Ohio

I make this dessert for birds that visit our place in winter. It helps replace the energy they're burning as they try to stay warm.

> *2 quarts water*
> *1 cup lard*

Brenda Klosse

"Birdmeal" attracts woodpeckers (like the two male pileated woodpeckers above). Mix 1 cup each of shortening, peanut butter and flour. Then mix in 4 cups of cornmeal. When finished, it should be the consistency of putty.

Press the mixture into the bark of trees and in the corners of your bird feeders.

—Harold Weppler
Atlantic, Iowa

> *4 cups dry cereal*
> *1 cup peanut butter*
> *Wheat germ, birdseed, sunflower*
> *seeds or wheat bran, optional*

Bring water and lard to a boil. Add cereal and cook for 15 minutes. Remove from heat and mix in peanut butter and optional ingredients.

Line plastic containers with plastic wrap and fill with the mixture. Place in freezer so it sets.

We'll often press the mixture into pinecones and hang them from tree branches near our picture windows.

—Nancy Wakeland
Entiat, Washington

You can shape this easy mixture into balls and serve it to backyard birds right away…there's no need to bake it.

1 cup peanut butter
1/2 cup cornmeal
1/4 cup honey
1/4 cup raisins
1/4 cup birdseed or peanut hearts
Water

Mix all the ingredients (except for water) in a large bowl. Add water slowly until mixture is workable, then form into 1-inch balls and serve on a tray feeder.

—*Matthew Dorfsmith*
Big Bear City, California

Here's a great recipe for filling log feeders. Just press the mixture into the feeder holes.

2 cups white flour
2 cups whole wheat flour
2 cups cornmeal
2 cups quick-cooking oats
1 teaspoon salt
2 cups shortening
1 cup lard
1-3/4 cups water

Combine the flours, cornmeal, oats and salt in a large bowl, kneading it with your hands. Add the shortening and lard and mix well. Then add enough water to make a stiff dough.

Divide the dough into smaller portions and store them in your freezer in plastic bags.

—*Carrollyn Poenie*
Louisville, Kentucky

ASK GEORGE

Finches and thrashers loved the large blocks of mixed seed I hung in mesh bags… but the store where I bought the seed blocks stopped carrying them. I'd like to make my own, but I don't know what will hold the seeds together in our hot climate. Can you give me some advice? —*Bernice Quiram*
Sun City, Arizona

George: There is a way to make seed blocks that will hold together in hot weather. I tried this recipe at home to make blocks like the one the downy woodpecker is feeding on in the photo (above). It works pretty well.

To make one seed block, add two 1/2-ounce envelopes of unflavored gelatin to 1/4 cup of water in a saucepan. Stir over low heat until the gelatin is completely dissolved and the water is clear.

Then stir in 1-1/4 cups of any combination of seeds that birds in your yard enjoy. Mix well so they all get coated with gelatin. Pack the mixture firmly into a plastic container and chill until solid. Remove it from the container, and it's ready for the birds!

Chapter 5
Hummingbird Havens

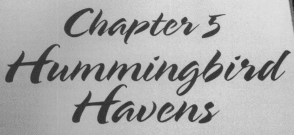

Framing my balcony on the 10th floor
I endorse the policy of an "open door".
On my dining table covered with lace,
Regal lilies filled a vase.
One day as I sat, let the cool breeze blow,
I saw a hummingbird darting to-and-fro.
Into my room
I saw him zoom
And into the flowers his bill he thrust,
Then quickly withdrew in deep disgust.
His rapid exit was so fantastic:
Those big red flowers are made of plastic!

We couldn't think of a more fitting way to open this chapter than with this fun poem from reader Helen Margaret Wilson of Sacramento, California.

Her exuberant words, as well as the many hints that follow, indicate how captivated people are by nature's tiny miracles in the sky.

If you'd like to attract these winged wonders to a backyard hummingbird haven of your own, read on…the proof is in the nectar and the plants.

Photo: Maslowski Photo

Spread a thick coat of shortening on hummingbird feeder posts and the wire the feeder hangs from. Ants won't attempt to wade through the gooey barrier. —*Doris Schaefer Greenville, Illinois*

Provide several sugar-water feeders for hummingbirds, but make sure they're out of sight from each other. The males don't like to share. —*Roberta Mistretta Tucker, Georgia*

Although hummingbirds aren't often seen in our area, I was able to attract them with a little patience. I diligently changed the sugar water in my feeder every few days and planted lots of red tubular flowers, like petunias, nearby. I was lucky to host a male (above) and several female ruby-throated hummingbirds throughout the summer months. —*Phyllis Schantz Cherry Hill, New Jersey*

While hummingbirds are attracted to red flowers, there's no need to use red food coloring in homemade sugar water. A clear solution of 4 parts water to 1 part sugar works just fine—there's plenty of red on the outside of commercial feeders to attract the birds.

Don't forget to boil the solution for about 1 minute and let it cool before serving. Change the sugar water every 3 to 5 days so that it doesn't ferment and keep the leftovers in the refrigerator for up to 1 week. —*Gary Clark Knowlton, Quebec*

To keep ants and bees away from hummingbird feeders, apply a coat of Shaklee's Basic H on the feeder ports and hanger. —*Carol Arena Anderson, Indiana*

Each morning I visit my local coffee shop to pick up their used coffee grounds. I hang them in small fabric bags near my hummingbird feeders. The aroma rids the areas of ants. —*Anna Victoria Reich Albuquerque, New Mexico*

I attract hummingbirds by setting out pieces of cantaloupe and other melons. Not only do the hummers like the juicy fruit, but fruit flies are also attracted to it. This gives the birds even more to eat. —*Derek Albrecht St. Cloud, Minnesota*

I hang my hummingbird feeder from a branch in a shady area that's about 5 feet above the ground. The nectar stays fresh longer when it's in the shade, and the branch's height makes it easy for me to take the feeder down when it needs cleaning. —*Alice Nelson Beloit, Wisconsin*

We plant lots of pink chenille near our sugar-water feeders, as well as amaryllis, bee balm, oriental lilies and hibiscus. Hummingbirds love this variety of plants, which we have placed throughout our yard.
—*Becca Brasfield*
Burns, Tennessee

We keep our hummingbird feeders insect-free by cutting an "X" in the center of a plastic or aluminum angel food cake pan. Slide it down the feeder pole and fill with water. It serves as a moat, stopping ants and june bugs in their tracks.
—*JoAnn Gaedke*
Westland, Michigan

We have a small pond in our backyard with a waterfall that produces a light mist. The hummingbirds love to whiz through the mist and drink from the pond. What a bonus!
—*Helen Miller*
Evant, Texas

I hang my hummingbird feeders from a plant hook that's attached to a shepherd's hook. The problem was that ants always found the sweet nectar before the flying jewels did.

So I smeared a thick layer of bacon grease on the plant hook. The ants won't cross the grease, so they now leave my feeder alone.
—*B. Beauregard*
Browns Mills, New Jersey

IT'S A FACT...
The inside diameters of most hummingbird nests are roughly the size of a quarter.

I've found that glass hummingbird feeders (like the one above) are easier to clean and stay that way longer. So the hummers never have to wait for their nectar, I have a clean feeder waiting in the wings to replace the one that needs scrubbing.
—*Billie Davis*
Lake Havasu City, Arizona

Hummingbirds seem to enjoy my sugar-water feeders more since I attached a plastic coffee can lid to the bottom of the feeders using epoxy. The lid serves as a perch, allowing the tiny birds to rest as they eat.
—*Klaus Bandle*
Malden, Massachusetts

Hang a hummingbird feeder from the same hook as a hanging basket of impatiens. By doing this, the hummingbirds enjoy a double treat.
—*Cynthia Hilton*
Nobleboro, Maine

Taller nectar-producing plants are the trick to attracting hummingbirds. My canna lilies, which are about as tall as I am, seem to be one of their favorite flowers to feed from.
—*Barbara Mohr*
Elkhorn, Wisconsin

My children (that's Emily with me above) and I learned that if we rest our fingers on the perches of our hummingbird feeders, the birds will readily light on them as they drink the sugar water. This experience is amazing! —*Debbie Eberting Clinton, Missouri*

We attract hummingbirds with *Monarda* (bee balm) and red carnations. They also visit my hanging baskets of begonias.
—*Marcia Briggs Pittsburgh, Pennsylvania*

In my garden, hummingbirds enjoy morning glories, four-o'clocks, gladiola, perennial sweet peas, lantana and Turk's cap lily.
—*Marsha Melder Shreveport, Louisiana*

I prefer attracting hummingbirds with nectar-producing plants rather than messing with making homemade sugar-water solutions.

One of their favorite plants is fuchsia, which hangs near our patio. It gives us a chance to get a close look

at these fascinating creatures.
In July, our hostas, red salvia and lavender begin to bloom, providing these birds with even more nectar.
—*Mrs. Glen Lambright Topeka, Indiana*

I plant sunflowers, zinnias and Mexican sunflowers (*tithonia*) to attract hummingbirds. Having plenty of water available for them also helps, especially if you have a mister. —*Ella Lucas Roanoke, Virginia*

To keep aphids away from your rosebushes without using chemicals, hang a hummingbird feeder above them. I tried this and was delighted with the results. The birds cleaned the bushes of every single aphid before they moved on to the feeder.
—*Joanne Craft-Lane Sumter, South Carolina*

Hummingbirds use dandelion seeds to line their nests, so I let these weeds go in my backyard. I also have discovered hummingbirds love nectar from Mexican sunflower, marigolds, periwinkle, lantana, cosmos, morning glories and impatiens.
—*Louise Grant Fort White, Florida*

IT'S A FACT...
Nectar feeders are not only popular with hummingbirds, but many other birds use them, too, including orioles, tanagers, catbirds and verdins.

ASK GEORGE

Last year I put out three hummingbird feeders. From early June through mid-October, four hummingbirds regularly visited the feeders. This year I hung four feeders and didn't see any hummers. I thought that once they visited, they continue to appear year after year. Any idea why they haven't? —Lyn Manson
Dallas, Texas

George: It's true that hummingbirds usually return to backyard feeders year after year. But the four hummers you saw may not have survived the long trip to the tropics and back. That would mean other hummers will have to find your feeders. When they do, you can expect them to reappear every spring.

My cypress vine, roses and gladiola are hummingbird favorites. They also like squash, pumpkin and cucumber flowers. They seem to go for anything yellow or red, so I plant lots of sunflowers and salvia for them, too. —Rita Jemison
Ashland, Mississippi

I haven't seen a single plant attract hummingbirds more than our potted Million Bells "petunia". Combined with a sugar-water feeder, we've created the perfect hummingbird haven. —Sharon Bohdan
Greenfield, Wisconsin

I attach a handheld watering wand to a trellis that's covered with trumpet vine. The hummingbirds can't resist zipping through the shower of water. —Gloria Meredith
Harrington, Delaware

Several of our western hummingbirds often build nests in blackberry vines and lilac bushes. So I plant nectar-producing plants, such as non-invasive honeysuckle and fuchsia, nearby to encourage these tiny gems to nest. —Liz McCain
Florence, Oregon

When my husband and I moved into a new home, we missed the hummingbirds that faithfully came to our old residence. To quickly attract the pretty birds to our new place, I tied 4-inch pieces of fluorescent ribbon to the wire hangers and perches of each hummingbird feeder in the yard. Within a week, we attracted several of these winged jewels. —Barbara Bennett
Olive Branch, Mississippi

Wasps are pests at my hummingbird feeders. But I've resolved the problem with cooking oil.

Each time I clean out my feeder, I dip my finger in oil and rub it around the feeding ports. It works—my feeders have been wasp-free for 4 years. —Betty Rochester
Pine Bluff, Arkansas

Hummingbirds can't resist bee balm (*Monarda*), especially the varieties that produce red flowers. It's extremely easy to grow and expands rapidly. To contain it, just plant it in an area with garden edging.

—*Deb Frie*
Melrose, Minnesota

My mom and dad, Delbert and Sibyl Alcorn, came up with this nifty stand to hang their hummingbird feeders from in the garden. They call it a "hummer trapeze".

It's just pieces of PVC pipe joined in a ladder-like shape and

held together with some adhesive. They drilled holes in the top crossbar and added hooks to hang their feeders. Now they can really enjoy these aerial acrobats! —*Jan McPheeters*
Kilgore, Texas

I planted fern-leaf lavender (*Lavandula multifida*) this spring and was amazed by how popular it was with hummingbirds.

With grayish-green foliage and long-blooming spikes that shoot up all summer, this is a perfect plant for a container garden.

—*Linda Schaffner*
Henderson, Nevada

Gold-flame honeysuckle vine attracts loads of hummingbirds. They prefer its nectar-producing flowers to the sugar water in hummingbird feeders. —*Bev Burgett*
Grass Lake, Michigan

Hyacinth bean vine is the perfect companion to sunflowers. The sunflowers' strong stalks support the vines, which in turn provide a great nectar-filled meal for hummingbirds. And at the end of summer, the sunflower heads mature and feed the other birds. —*Lena Lantz*
Strasburg, Pennsylvania

If you live on the migratory path of hummingbirds, the best way to attract them is to put up lots of feeders before they arrive. In our area, that's in late February when they're moving north and in late August when they're flying back to their winter grounds.

I routinely put out about nine feeders, filling them with only small amounts of sugar water until I see the first arrivals. Then I'll fill them to the brim.

Through my yearly observations, I can just about predict when the tiny birds will arrive. In fact, they'll

often come on the winds of a front and leave the same way. So it pays to watch the weather forecast.
—*Dale Thomas, Humble, Texas*

Keep hummingbird feeders ant-free by spraying their hangers with a coat of multipurpose white lithium grease. One application lasts about a month and completely eliminates the problem. —*Ron O'Brien Glendora, California*

Dominant male hummingbirds often chase other flying jewels that visit the sugar-water feeders in my backyard. But I've discovered that by moving one feeder out of the hummingbird's line of sight, the problem has been eliminated.
—*Vivian Vican Claryville, New York*

Here's a quick and simple hummingbird nectar recipe that should save you time in the kitchen. Just mix 1 cup of sugar with 1 cup of water and bring it to a boil until the sugar dissolves. Turn off the heat and add 1 tray of ice cubes (my full tray equals 1 cup of water, but I suggest that you check yours first) and stir until they're melted. Then stir

> **IT'S A FACT...**
> Ruby-throated hummingbirds build their small, cup-shaped nests about 10 to 20 feet above the ground.

in 2 cups cold water. Now you can fill your feeders. It takes less than 5 minutes from start to finish.
—*Lorna Hardin Garden Valley, California*

One afternoon I hung a wet shirt out on my porch so it would dry. When I went to retrieve it, the shirt had accidently slipped off the wire hanger and onto the ground. In the shirt's place was a precious ruby-throated hummingbird perched on the hanger, which was near my hummingbird feeder. I left the hanger there and have been blessed with numerous repeat visits from hummingbirds. They like to perch there before and after eating.
—*Lucinda Chamblee Summerville, Georgia*

For a hummingbird-friendly yard, plant lots of penta flowers near your sugar-water feeders.
—*Doris Allen, Houston, Texas*

By George... Keep nectar feeders up through autumn. It's not food that determines when hummingbirds will migrate, but the amount of sunlight. In fact, it's a good idea to leave feeders up as late as possible to give the birds a good nutritional start for their journey. —*George Harrison Contributing Editor*

When the hummingbirds return to our place in spring, they're usually hungry from their long migration. To help them replenish their energy, I keep my sugar-water feeders full and offer them a buffet of fruit—apples, oranges, grapefruits, kiwifruit and pears, to name a few.

I've seen them eat all of these fruits, but they're especially fond of oranges and kiwi.

As a bonus, the fruit will also attract a variety of other birds in your yard, many of which you usually don't see at bird feeders.
—Kimberly Bestys
Hammondsport, New York

Tie bright-pink lengths of survey tape (available at most hardware stores) to hummingbird feeders and throughout your yard. This definitely attracts the tiny birds. Be sure to provide several nectar feeders to keep one male from dominating all the others. *—Sharon Posey*
Alabaster, Alabama

I've discovered hummingbirds enjoy any kind of lily. The trumpet- shape flowers light up the yard and invite the beautiful birds to my home. *—Theresa Beck*
Galveston, Indiana

Cypress vine is an excellent plant for attracting hummingbirds. It grows quickly and blooms with plentiful red flowers.
—Mrs. Everette Scheffel
Pryor, Oklahoma

I place red artificial flowers directly below my hummingbird feeders. The birds might not notice the sugar water at first, but once they realize the blooms are fake, it doesn't take long for them to investigate the feeders. *—Carol Woodland*
Annapolis Royal, Nova Scotia

Feeding hummingbirds used to be a chore, but here are some shortcuts I've learned over the years that have made it easier:

• *Homemade nectar*—When you make a sugar-water solution (4 parts water to 1 part sugar, boil and cool), make a large batch. After the solution completely cools, measure how

---

ASK GEORGE

Why do the hummingbirds around our sugar-water feeders act so aggressive? There's plenty of room for several to feed at once, but one often chases the others away. *—Matthew Welch*
Hyrum, Utah

George: There's usually a dominant male hummingbird that controls which birds feed from sugar-water feeders and flower beds in its territory. Females that are sociable with the dominant male usually are allowed to feed, while other males and females are sent packing.

much liquid is needed to fill your feeder and pour equal amounts into resealable freezer bags.

As I need a refill, I simply remove a bag from the freezer and thaw it on the counter or in the microwave. Then just pour it into the feeder.

• *Cleaning*—Sometimes black mold forms inside my hummingbird feeders. To clean them, I simply break up a denture-cleaning tablet and add it to the reservoir with plain water.

After the tablet does its work, I thoroughly rinse the feeder. If stubborn stains remain, add a tablespoon of salt to plain water in the feeder and shake vigorously. The grains of salt will scrub the reservoir. I like these methods because they're nontoxic.

• *Pesky ants*—Here in Texas, fire ants are a terrible problem. They raid and clog my feeders so hummingbirds can't feed.

Again, I've discovered a simple nontoxic remedy. I spray the feeder's hanger with a light coat of nonstick cooking spray. Ants don't like this spray, but it doesn't seem to bother the hummingbirds.

—*Walter Norvell*
Fort Worth, Texas

My nectar recipe uses the traditional 4 parts water to 1 part sugar, but I also add a teaspoon of vanilla

extract. The extra flavoring is a hummingbird favorite. They'll even begin feeding just as I back away from the feeders.

—*Alice Davis Merker*
Newton, Georgia

I add red buttons and beads to our hummingbird feeders. As you can see (above), they float in the sugar water, creating an extra attraction for the little birds. There's a practical purpose to this as well. At a glance I can tell when a feeder needs filling. —*Hank Baker*
Frankfort, Kentucky

Hummingbirds used to fight for spots at my sugar-water feeders until they drove each other out of my yard completely. So I took down my feeders and concentrated on planting red flowers. Now, the birds have returned and peacefully feed on nectar from my pentas, hibiscus and roses. —*Laura Oakes*
Eustis, Florida

IT'S A FACT...
Each hummingbird egg—there's usually two or three eggs in a clutch—is just 1/2 inch long.

Here in central Canada, the hummingbirds usually arrive before the flowers bloom. To ensure

I use the typical recipe for hummingbird nectar (1 part sugar to 4 parts water) but have a few helpful hints to keep the hummingbird fuel in tip-top condition:

• Mix the sugar with boiling water for about 1 minute to help dissolve the sugar. Wait until it's cool before filling the feeder.

• Keep excess sugar water in the refrigerator so it doesn't spoil. It'll keep for up to a week.

• There's no need to color the sugar water. Most feeders have plenty of red to attract hummingbirds.

• Change the sugar water in feeders every 2 or 3 days.

• If you spot mildew in the feeder, empty it and thoroughly clean it before refilling.

• Plant red flowers nearby to attract hummingbirds.
                            —John Hillman
                            Cape Fair, Missouri

they'll be well fed, we start filling our sugar-water feeders in early spring, so they have plenty of food when they arrive from their long journey.   *—Marion King*
                            Gloucester, Ontario

I've discovered an easy solution to a hummingbird-feeder problem that many people don't even know about. When filling feeders with sugar water, they sometimes become air locked, which means a bubble forms in the feeding ports, keeping the food from flowing.

To prevent this, simply tap the feeder a few times when you fill it, and the air bubbles will loosen and rise to the top. We tap our hummingbird feeders whenever we pass by them, which keeps our sugar water flowing.   *—Grace Ragsdale*
                            Cambridge, Ohio

Place dried cattail stalks out for the hummingbirds. I've seen a female hummingbird pull out bits of the cattail down to use as nesting material. In fact, these old cattails attract more hummingbird activity to my yard than any flower or feeder.
                            —Tom Godin
            100 Mile House, British Columbia

I bring all my sugar-water feeders indoors every 4 days for a good cleaning. I use hot water and a couple drops of vinegar to keep mold from invading the tiny feeding ports. I also use a baby-bottle brush to scrub them out. Always rinse thoroughly with hot water.
                            —Gloria Meredith
                            Harrington, Delaware

Be sure to sweep away large spiderwebs hanging below your roof eaves near hummingbird feeders. I found a tiny hummingbird entangled in an especially large web.
—*Pauline Mount*
Enosburg Falls, Vermont

Hang red ribbons or a red hand towel near your hummingbird feeders to attract these birds' attention. Once they see red, they'll find your feeder in a hurry.
—*Tina Jacobs*
Wantage, New Jersey

I plant peas on trellises between my nectar feeders. This seems to deter hummingbirds from claiming the feeders as their own because it helps prevent visual contact between the birds. The pea blossoms also provide an additional source of nectar.
—*Jim Low*
Jefferson City, Missouri

Keeping my sugar-water feeders clean was a chore until I discovered this simple solution:

In a large pail with gentle laun-

IT'S A FACT...
Hang a banana peel near sugar-water feeders. Fruit flies will flock to the skin, and hummingbirds will gladly feast on the protein-rich visitors.

---

dry detergent and water (follow the manufacturer's directions for proportions), immerse the dirty feeder for about an hour, brush it clean and rinse it well.

It does the trick. All the scum comes right off.
—*Mrs. Fred Rahn*
Center City, Minnesota

When I boil eggs, I save the water to make hummingbird nectar. It gives the birds an extra boost of calcium that's especially helpful during nesting season.

Add 1/4 cup sugar to each cup of "egg water". Boil the mixture again so the sugar dissolves well, let it cool and pour it into a clean hummingbird feeder.
—*Barbara Cogburn*
Clyde, North Carolina

In an attempt to be thrifty, I made a hummingbird feeder from a 12-ounce juice bottle and a straw.

Simply cut the straw to a length of 1-1/2 inches and cut a small hole the diameter of the straw about 1/2 inch from the bottom of the bottle.

Insert the straw into the hole, placing it at about a 45° upward angle. Use waterproof glue to hold the straw in place.

Now fill the bottle with the usual 4 to 1 ratio of sugar water while holding your finger over the straw as you fill the bottle and cap it.

Tie a red ribbon around the neck of the bottle and viola—a hummingbird feeder!
—*Patty Roberts, Springville, Utah*

Pink coral bells and columbine are hummingbird favorites in our yard. Since we live within their migration path, we've made sure we plant plenty of these coveted flowers. —*Frank Boster Jr. Delaware, Ohio*

A hummingbird had been repeatedly visiting my garage and refused to leave. I noticed it would land on the emergency-release cord for the garage door opener, which had a red handle. So I covered the handle with black electrical tape, and the hummingbird left. I haven't had a problem since. —*Joe Chincheck Wheeling, West Virginia*

Leave hummingbird feeders filled with fresh nectar for a few weeks after most hummers have left for the winter. Hummingbirds passing through will welcome your feeders. —*Connie Garland Greenwood, Indiana*

Saved by the Net

WHEN I OPENED the door to our garage, I heard a strange and unfamiliar noise. Up near the rafters, I spotted a hummingbird darting back and forth, trying to find its way out.

"How will I lure this tiny bird to safety?" I wondered. My husband, Ron, suggested we turn to the Internet.

With a few clicks, we found *www.hummingbirds.net*. There on the opening page in bold letters it said, "A hummingbird was trapped in my garage! Try this rescue technique." My heart leaped with joy.

With a click, I found out that this was a fairly common problem. You see, hummingbirds often are attracted to the red emergency-release handles on automatic garage door openers. After discovering the handles hold no nectar, the birds fly up near the ceiling and are trapped.

The Web site instructed us to get a flashlight, close the garage door and turn off the overhead lights when the hummingbird flies over a clear section of the garage floor.

Because hummingbirds have poor night vision, they can't find a place to perch in the darkness and will flutter to the ground.

Sure enough—the hummingbird landed safely. We used the flashlight to help locate our little friend, and Ron scooped it up and carried it outside.

The Web site had one last tip—paint emergency pulls a dark color or at least hide them out of sight. I painted ours that very evening. —*Sharon Hanson Coralville, Iowa*

I attract hummingbirds to my backyard with nectar-rich flowers. Some of their favorites are *Salvia guaranitica*, a blue tubular flower, and *Silene regia*, also known as royal catchfly. —*Renee Benage St. Louis, Missouri*

Several hummingbirds have mistakenly flown into my house. I've helped them escape by placing a tall potted plant (if possible, a nectar-producing plant) near the doorway. They're drawn to the protection of the foliage and soon find their way back into the fresh air. —*Pam White, Huntsville, Alabama*

Hummingbirds visit my backyard during the summer, but not until my patch of red flowers begins blooming. So I attract the first birds returning from their winter grounds to my sugar-water feeders by placing artificial flowers in my planters. As soon as the weather warms enough for me to plant annuals, I'll replace them with fresh flowers. —*Terry Zander Thurmont, Maryland*

Hummingbirds sometimes fly into my garage and get stuck. To help them out, I just place a pot of bright-red flowers in the doorway. This method hasn't failed yet! —*Georgia Dummers Winfield, West Virginia*

When making homemade sugar water for hummingbirds, never use honey as a substitute for sugar. The honey ferments rapidly and actually speeds up mold formation.

ASK GEORGE
I've heard hummingbirds sometimes hitch rides on the backs of geese as they migrate. Is this true?
—*Eva Hetherington Ninette, Manitoba*

George: Sometimes legends never die, and the one about hummingbirds hitching rides on Canada geese is one of them. It's based on an early 20th-century report about a hunter who killed a Canada goose and allegedly found a hummingbird in its feathers.

The bottom line is that hummingbirds and Canada geese migrate at different times of the year and to different destinations. So it would not make sense for a hummingbird to stow away on a goose.

In addition, artificial sweeteners should never be used, and red coloring isn't necessary—most hummingbird feeders have plenty of red on them to attract these winged miracles. —*Angela Griffin Hatchett Altoona, Alabama*

Since hummingbirds flock toward the color red, I removed the red cap from a whipped cream can, filled it with hummingbird nectar and held it in my hand. It didn't take long before I got a close-up view of these amazing birds.
—Pauline Yeaton
Farmington, Maine

I found that just about anything red that holds water will work as a hummingbird feeder. For example, when I was in a pinch one spring, I used a red soup ladle filled with sugar water as a feeder. I just fastened it to a porch post with electrical tape and watch the winged wonders feed.
—Phyllis Meyer
Franklin Springs, New York

I formed an arched trellis out of a 16-foot length of hog wire and planted morning glories and cardinal climbers on it. The hummingbirds especially like this pretty nectar-producing planting.
—Jacque Hodson, Ackworth, Iowa

One afternoon while I was gathering fragrant nasturtiums to display on our kitchen table, I noticed a hummingbird was trying to get to the plant's blooms. However, the canopy of green leaves covering the flowers

> **IT'S A FACT...**
> The brightly colored throat patches on male hummingbirds are called gorgets.

kept it from reaching the nectar.

So I held out my colorful bouquet, hoping the hummer would enjoy a few sips. Surprisingly, the tiny winged wonder accepted the invitation. It visited nearly every bloom, and I got a remarkably close-up look at this small miracle.
—Nancy Omernick
Stevens Point, Wisconsin

Try planting a scarlet sage (red salvia) and standing cypress (Texas plume) if you want to attract flocks of hummingbirds.   *—Lois Minosky*
Zanesville, Ohio

I live in the Southeast, so the only hummingbird we regularly see is the ruby-throated species. But I read that rufous hummingbirds may stop in our area late in the year. So I continued to fill my nectar feeders well into winter. You can imagine my excitement when I saw my first rufous hummingbird stop by for a drink. Now, I keep the feeders filled all year.   *—Kem Willis*
Effingham, South Carolina

> **By George...** Hummingbirds can sometimes be spotted hanging upside down from a feeder perch or tree branch. They can shut down their metabolism to conserve energy. This condition, called "torpidity", is normal and shouldn't cause you to worry about the flying jewel.
> *—George Harrison, Contributing Editor*

While my yard blooms with dozens of red, pink and orange tubular flowers that hummingbirds love, some of the most productive flowers that attract these winged wonders to my yard are red columbine, coral bell, Canterbury bell, cardinal flower, fuchsia, hollyhocks, impatiens, phlox and red salvia.
—*Gloria Meredith*
Harrington, Delaware

While I realize hummingbirds are particularly attracted to red flowers, I've found that a planter containing red and a variety of other colors of the same type of nectar-producing flower is also beneficial. I've noticed some of the birds will visit yellow blooms first, while others prefer to stop at purple.
—*Joan Book*
Jackson, New Jersey

I use monofilament fishing line to hang my hummingbird feeders after I discovered it's too slippery for ants to scale. Now, I don't worry about the tiny pests contaminating the sugar water. —*Tim Ward*
Centreville, Maryland

Hummingbirds weren't visiting the feeder I had hung by my large picture window. So I relocated it near some protective vines and shrubs. Then, as they became accustomed to the feeder, we slowly moved it closer to our window until it was placed in the ideal viewing spot. This method works—we love to watch these beautiful birds.
—*John and Vi Howe*
Miles City, Montana

Here's how to make a handheld hummingbird feeder from household items (see photo above). Glue a red fabric or plastic flower to the top of a film canister and pierce a hole through both the flower and lid. Fill the canister with sugar water, cap it up and remove your active hummingbird feeder. Then stand still and wait for the jewels to discover your treat. —*Betty Pierce*
Slaterville Springs, New York

Hang wire coat hangers near sugar-water feeders. The hummingbirds perch on the hangers to wait their turn at the feeder and sometimes even preen themselves there.
—*Karen Laabs*
Spokane, Washington

IT'S A FACT...
To match a hummingbird's voracious appetite, a 180-pound person would need to consume about 190 Big Macs and Super-size fries in 1 day!

In early spring, I hang red plastic lids from raisin canisters near my nectar feeders and from plants that produce red flowers. This attracts the attention of hummingbirds so they know where to "come and get it".   —*Anna Victoria Reich*
Albuquerque, New Mexico

My brother-in-law, John Dummert, solved the annoying problem of ants on his hummingbird feeder with this clever device.

He slid a plastic funnel onto the shepherd's hook where he hangs his feeder. The funnel is about halfway up the hook, held into place with some watertight plumber's putty.

John keeps the funnel filled with water, and now he—and the area hummers—enjoy an ant-free feeder.   —*Beth Petre*
Oak Creek, Wisconsin

My wife, Linda, and I have developed a fun way to view hummingbirds up close.

We took a wire coat hanger, bent it into a "cup holder" and attached it to an old red baseball hat (that's Linda wearing it above). Then we secured a red plastic bottle top upside down at the far end of the holder and filled it with sugar water.

When we don the hat, we get a real bird's-eye view of the hungry hummers.   —*Tommy Crawford*
Yorktown, Indiana

The sugar-water feeders that receive the most visitors in my yard are the ones with red plastic flowers at the feeding ports. Since hummers are drawn to red flowers, it only makes sense they would find these feeders first.

If your feeder doesn't have flowers, simply attach a plastic or fabric bloom near the feeding port.
—*Julie Smith, Medina, Ohio*

Chapter 6
Perfect Plantings

*T*here isn't a better way to liven or brighten up your backyard than with flowers, shrubs and trees that put out the welcome mat for winged activity.

With the right selections, these plantings become even more colorful and attractive as birds flock to their berries, seeds and protective branches.

To create a bird-watching bonanza, try some of these reader-tested "perfect plantings". With their colorful combinations, you'll be offering a backyard buffet for your feathered friends.

Photo: Carolyn Chatterton

The Kentucky blueberry, as it's called around here, is the perfect plant for birds. (Its botanical name is *Mahonia*.) This shrub has prickly leaves similar to holly, so it makes a great protective hiding place for songbirds.

It also produces fragrant yellow flowers in spring, followed by a smorgasbord of large berries. Eastern bluebirds, American robins, wood thrushes, cedar waxwings, brown thrashers, tufted titmice and northern cardinals flock to my yard to feed on its fruit. —*Lisa Kimmich*
Athens, Georgia

To provide winter sustenance for birds, I make sure to keep plenty of rosebushes and spirea shrubs in my garden (below). A variety of feathered friends stop to dine on

the rose hips and spirea seeds after other food sources have been eaten or disappeared. —*Inga Burkholder*
Cecil Lake, British Columbia

I stopped killing dandelions in my yard after my aunt reminded me that many birds are attracted to the bright blossoms. In fact, many birds eat the seeds of these pesky weeds—nature's way of controlling them. —*Elaine Massie*
Fayetteville, West Virginia

Hummingbirds like my cypress vines, roses and gladiolus, as well as squash, pumpkin and cucumber flowers. —*Rita Jemison*
Ashland, Mississippi

Plant trumpet and honeysuckle vines to keep hummingbirds and other nectar eaters, like orioles, tanagers, warblers and woodpeckers, happy. —*Georgia Stewart*
Hebron, Illinois

Plant liatris in your garden. These perennials easily grow from seed, producing pretty purple flowers that the birds love. They often cling to the spiky blooms to eat the seeds.
—*Verna Olson*
Fargo, North Dakota

Chickadees feed on the seeds from the huge sunflowers I plant throughout my backyard. I leave the stalks standing all winter so the little birds can continue stopping by for snacks. —*Linda Borasio-Wolfe*
Parma, Ohio

By placing feeders near my garden, birds are more likely to eat pesky insects that damage my vegetables. —*Alice Nelson*
Beloit, Wisconsin

When I was young, I'd crush the petals of touch-me-nots and add them to water to make a sweet perfume. Now that I have this plant in my own garden, I've noticed hum-

mingbirds and butterflies are attracted to its nectar as well.
—*Rebecca King*
Burlison, Tennessee

Birds can't resist the clusters of berries that hang from my viburnum shrub. —*Barbara Manheim*
New Lenox, Illinois

My husband attaches cedar branches to our bird feeder posts. These serve as perches where birds can wait their turn to feed and also provide protection from predators. Plus, they give a lovely natural appearance to the feeding station.
—*Barb Peachey*
Denver, Pennsylvania

When I noticed the caterpillars in my dill patch attracted a pair of red-eyed vireos, I stopped trying to protect my dill from the nibblers. I've also seen eastern bluebirds and yellow-billed cuckoos feeding on the caterpillars as well. —*Jim Low*
Jefferson City, Missouri

Cedar trees near our feeders provide great cover while the birds eat. We make sure to trim the branches several feet off the ground so preda-

tors like cats can't lurk beneath them. —*Becca Brasfield*
Burns, Tennessee

My neighbor's Washington hawthorn is ideal for birds. Its red berries provide winter nourishment

and its thorns deter cats. Plus, the tree's branches are the perfect height for hanging birdhouses.
—*Jo Ann Sheldon*
Arkansas City, Kansas

I attract eastern bluebirds to my yard with a variety of plantings. Sumac, flowering dogwood, grape, non-invasive honeysuckle, climbing bittersweet, pokeweed and greenbriar seem to be their favorites.
—*Angela Griffin Hatchett*
Altoona, Alabama

My mulberry tree is the perfect combination of blooms and berries. In early spring it produces pretty blossoms, followed by thousands of berries in summer. The birds simply adore it—and so do I. American robins seem especially appreciative of its luscious bounty.
—*Ed Toner Jr.*
Howell, New Jersey

IT'S A FACT...
Attract northern mockingbirds by planting blackberry, dogwood, mulberry, grape, juniper and serviceberry. In desert areas, try prickly pear cactus—they can't resist its fruits.

When I make gourd birdhouses, I personalize them by using a ball-point pen to scratch names into the gourds while they're still on the vine. As the gourd grows, the name does, too. It's a fun way to keep track of the birds in our yard. We just refer to them by the name on the house. —*Roberta Witteman Nampa, Idaho*

I often see American goldfinches flocking around my cosmos—especially in autumn as the plants go to seed. I've counted at least a dozen finches bouncing from one stem to another in search of seeds.
—*Cherie Boulton Hayward, California*

Plant bachelor's buttons (below) if you want to see more American goldfinches in your yard. The bright-yellow birds flock to the

flowers and create a striking contrast against the delicate blue and white blooms. —*Louise Daugherty Bethel, Missouri*

My hawthorn tree has lovely white blossoms in spring and clusters of bright-red berries in fall. Northern cardinals simply love it— I've often spotted males plucking berries to feed to their mates.
—*Alice Nelson, Beloit, Wisconsin*

To attract woodpeckers, I "planted" a dead tree in my yard and turned it into a bird buffet.

I drilled 1-inch holes along the trunk and filled them with suet and peanut butter. Then I attached a few nails and hung orange and apple halves on them.

If you choose a tree about the same diameter as a telephone pole, the woodpeckers may even nest in it. But let them bore their own holes!
—*Tonja Karnes Hopkins, Michigan*

To give birds a place to perch in my garden, I set up a small post and attached a branch at its top. Now birds often sit there to survey the area, occasionally darting out after flying insects. —*Harry Bowden Olive Branch, Mississippi*

To attract winged activity to our large peony beds, we sprinkle cosmos seeds among them. This also will extend your garden's show of color—cosmos continue to bloom long after peonies have finished.
—*Lillian Zemmin Grosse Pointe Woods, Michigan*

Nothing brings in the birds like our crab apple trees. Northern mockingbirds, American robins, cedar waxwings and others eat the fruits.
　　　　　—Charlotte Clark
　　　　　Glenpool, Oklahoma

Encourage frequent visits from American robins by planting dogwood and sumac. The cheery birds spend a lot of time in these shrubs in my yard.　　　*—Liz McCain*
　　　　　Florence, Oregon

American goldfinches flock to the seeds of our liatris.
—Gary Clark, Knowlton, Quebec

I've found sunflowers, marigolds and cosmos attract lots of seed-eating birds, including the brightly colored American goldfinches.
　　　　　—Tina Jacobs
　　　　　Wantage, New Jersey

I've discovered Montana bluets and zinnias (pictured above) provide food for American goldfinches. The birds bend the drying flower heads to the ground as they land on them, then pull out the seeds with their bills. It's fascinating to watch.
　　　　　—Charlene Margetiak
　　　　　Norwalk, Ohio

Since I started planting perennial bachelor's buttons and purple coneflower in my yard, I've seen more American goldfinches than ever before.　　　*—Jill Hersch*
　　　　　Ayr, North Dakota

When our old silver maple tree died, we decided to cut it down, except for 15 feet of its trunk and branches. At first, it didn't look very good, but climbing hydrangea, Virginia creeper and English ivy soon spruced it up.

I also hung birdhouses from its limbs and spread peanut butter on the coarse bark. Now it's a favorite spot for birds to visit.　　*—Lori Qualls*
　　　　　Midland, Michigan

Brown thrashers visit my yard to feast on the ageratum, four-o'-clocks, hostas and cannas.
　　　　　—Marsha Melder
　　　　　Shreveport, Louisiana

Sparrows often gather around my red and yellow trumpet vines. They even huddle among the branches in winter to keep warm.
　　　　　—Bev Burgett
　　　　　Grass Lake, Michigan

Keep feathered friends coming to your backyard by planting a mix of trees and shrubs that will produce fruits and berries year-round, not all at the same time.   *—Emily Grey*
Onancock, Virginia

We've planted a variety of trees, shrubs and flowers in our yard, but the birds' favorites are the blueberries, hazelnuts, huckleberries, forget-me-nots and dogwood fruits.
—Shirley Van Mechelen
Everett, Washington

Choke cherry and cherry trees are a popular pick for American robins. I often watch as they pluck the ripe fruit (below), then wash it in my birdbath!   *—Anne Fauvell*
Rapid City, South Dakota

Northwest Cherry Growers

After a neighbor gave me a couple catnip plants, I placed them in my backyard near a fence. A few weeks later, I noticed they appeared quite bare, so I was going to pull them out. But a closer look revealed purple finches were busily stripping the plants of their leaves.

I decided to let the plants be— and they still attract lots of hungry birds!   *—Nancy Felch*
Beulah, North Dakota

Berry-loving birds are sure to flock to a mulberry tree. We planted ours in the backyard where its abundant fallen leaves and flower petals wouldn't bother our neighbors. It's worth the mess, however, when birds gather to eat the plentiful mulberries that form in summer.
—John and Eula Henline
Sioux City, Iowa

I've found two types of purple flowers that attract lots of winged activity—stokesia and liatris (sometimes called blazing star or gayfeather). Stokesia, also called stokes aster, looks like an annual aster with narrow purple petals extending upward. Liatris produces long spikes of blooms with green leaves shooting out from the main stalk.
—Gloria Meredith
Harrington, Delaware

My brother, Nathan, and I have noticed hummingbirds like to rest among the branches of our mulberry. We've also seen blue jays and northern mockingbirds eating its fruit.   *—Brian Jones*
Sweet Springs, Missouri

We provide plenty of cover for birds in our backyard with trees and shrubs. Our favorites are Norway spruce and yew. The birds flee to the dense branches when they sense danger.   *—Connie Garland*
Greenwood, Indiana

A few young apple trees didn't survive their first winter. So instead of removing them, I moved them near my bird feeders. Now they provide convenient perches while the birds wait their turn to eat. One day, I counted over 100 small birds at the feeders with plenty more waiting in the wings. —*Lin Lehmicke Luck, Wisconsin*

I have several mature mountain ash trees in my yard. But instead of letting the birds eat the berries when they ripen, I remove the fruit in fall and freeze them (sometimes as much as 50 pounds). Then I'll offer them at my bird feeders throughout winter. Both cedar and Bohemian waxwings flock to my yard for this unexpected treat. —*Robert Morin Lac-Saint-Charles, Quebec*

For more blue jays, try planting plumed cockscomb, marigolds, sunflowers (above), zinnias, four-o'clocks, hibiscus and gourds. —*Marsha Melder Shreveport, Louisiana*

Buntings and finches really love the tall spikes of blooms on our common mullein. This wildflower is just one of many carefree beauties that attract birds to our yard. —*Marcia Sinclair Marion, North Carolina*

ASK GEORGE

We recently moved to a new housing development where there are no trees. I'd like to put up birdhouses and feeders, but worry the lack of protective cover will keep birds from using them. How can I attract birds to such an open area? —*Charlotte Van Cassele Brockport, New York*

George: You're correct in assuming birds are unlikely to nest or feed in a backyard that doesn't have some protective natural cover. The solution is simple—you'll need to plant some.

Evergreens will give you instant cover, in summer or winter. So will a discarded Christmas tree or a pile of brush.

If the season is right for planting, you can add deciduous shrubs, shade trees and ground covers. Then the birds should flock to your yard to nest, eat and bathe.

If you spot a seed-bearing plant like pokeweed or pigweed sprouting near your compost heap, let it grow. Birds will use it as a natural food source.
—*Jim Low, Jefferson City, Missouri*

In winter, nandina, holly and juniper often hold on to their fruit—providing food for birds as the temperature drops.   —*Emily Grey Onancock, Virginia*

Our garden consists of 2 dozen rosebushes, as well as petunias, coral bells, spider plants, trumpet vine and ever-blooming weigela. These blossoms surround our quaint birdbath.

The combination of the blooms and birdbath create a perfect resting stop for hummingbirds and blue jays. In fact, on summer evenings, we sit on the porch and watch the birds just a few feet away!
—*M.L. Tomlinson North Vernon, Indiana*

Since I planted a pomegranate tree in my yard, I've noticed an increase in bird activity. In spring and summer, the tree's orange-red flowers attract hummingbirds. And come fall and early winter, a multitude of lovely red fruit appears.
—*Carol Ann Gensert Canoga Park, California*

My Burford holly (*Ilex cornuta 'Burfordii'*) is a favorite nesting place for northern mockingbirds. I grouped several together to provide all my backyard birds a safe haven.
—*Marsha Melder Shreveport, Louisiana*

Hugh P. Smith Jr.

To attract orioles to your yard, plant nectar-producing flowers like red-hot poker (right), as well as flowering and fruit-bearing trees and shrubs.
—*Allison Schott Brantford, Ontario*

I set aside a special corner of my yard just for the birds. Native vegetation supplies nectar, food and cover. And a small unplanted area is the perfect spot for "dust bathing", which helps birds remove parasites from their feathers.
—*Karin Arrigoni San Jose, California*

Plant pink and red azaleas, petunias and daylilies to attract hummingbirds. Their funnel-shaped nectar-producing blooms and bright hues will invite the winged jewels to your backyard. —*Laura Horning* *Mifflintown, Pennsylvania*

A pair of house finches build a nest in my blue spruce each spring. —*Connie Garland* *Greenwood, Indiana*

Thorny trees like Washington and other hawthorns provide excellent food and nesting sites. The spines help discourage potential predators. —*Jill Hersch* *Ayr, North Dakota*

My honeysuckle doesn't stop attracting birds when its flowers fade. Its succulent berries are a great attraction for cedar waxwings later in the season. Be careful to select only non-invasive species. Ask your local nursery or county Extension service for the best varieties for your area. —*Gary Clark* *Knowlton, Quebec*

I've had more visitors at my hummingbird feeders since I planted butterfly bush and trumpet vine near them. Now the brilliant birds empty the sugar-water feeders so quickly, I can hardly keep up! —*Marianne La Fountaine* *Fremont, Ohio*

I've found hummingbirds love columbine, coral bells and red and purple salvia. —*Georgia Stewart* *Hebron, Illinois*

My grandmother, Edwina Hilliard of Medina, Tennessee, gave me a mimosa tree. I treasure the tree because it reminds me of my childhood—I used to call its tiny feathery blooms "hula skirts". But I discovered an unexpected benefit. Hummingbirds are fond of its flowers' sweet nectar. —*Rebecca King* *Burlison, Tennessee*

I attract hummingbirds with hollyhocks and cannas. —*Sandra Voss* *Granville, Iowa*

After I cut down a tree on my property, I realized too late that it had been a favorite spot for a pileated woodpecker. So I decided to "plant" the trunk in a different area of my yard. Now woodpeckers continue to hammer on the dead tree. Maybe one day they'll even nest in it. —*Harold Koth* *Tomahawk, Wisconsin*

My weigela (like the showy one below) attracts lots of nectar-feeding birds. —*Theresa Maiorana* *Ashford, Connecticut*

87

The berries of my mountain ash are a favorite of cedar waxwings (below). After the leaves fall, the regal birds flock to my tree, staying until all the fruit is gone.

—*Bettie Pierce*
Slaterville Springs, New York

Hummingbirds often feed on the rudbeckia and coral bells in our garden.
—*Gary Clark*
Knowlton, Quebec

Plant geraniums, rose of Sharon and rhododendrons to attract hummingbirds.
—*Tina Jacobs*
Wantage, New Jersey

Ever since I added a beautiful trumpet honeysuckle in my yard, the hummingbirds haven't stopped coming. The plant blooms early in the growing season and produces deep-red nectar flowers well into late fall.
—*Sandy Collier*
Charlotte, North Carolina

Scarlet tanagers, indigo buntings, cedar waxwings, northern cardinals, house finches and American robins simply adore my serviceberries and dogwoods.
—*Bev Dennison*
Crandon, Wisconsin

We allow perennials to grow and reseed in one corner of our lot, attracting lots of pine siskins and finches.
—*Mrs. Les Demargerie*
Sprague, Manitoba

Border your backyard with trees and shrubs in a variety of types and sizes.

I plant large shade trees to create a

By George... I recommend the following "perfect plantings" for a backyard bird haven that's bustling with activity:

Shrubs:
Bayberry, blackberry, blueberry, cotoneaster, dogwood, elderberry, highbush cranberry, holly, non-invasive honeysuckle, huckleberry, juniper, mandrone, manzanita, mulberry, prickly pear, raspberry, serviceberry, snowberry, spicebush, sumac, summer sweet, viburnum, virginia creeper, winterberry and wisteria.

Trees:
Ash, beech, blackgum, cedar, cherry, crab apple, dogwood, fir, hackberry, hawthorn, hemlock, maple, mesquite, mountain ash, oak, pine, spruce and walnut.
—*George Harrison, Contributing Editor*

canopy, shorter trees for additional perches, and shrubs underneath for shelter. This creates a habitat where birds can safely feed and bathe.

—*Karin Arrigoni*
San Jose, California

We've had a lot of hummingbirds in our backyard since we added bee balm, cardinal flower, morning glory and Dropmore Scarlet honeysuckle (pictured below). An added bonus is the honeysuckle blooms from early spring until frost.

—*Barbara Mohr*
Elkhorn, Wisconsin

In my garden, the hummingbirds enjoy morning glories (above), four-o'clocks, orange and red gladiolus, perennial sweet peas, lantana and turkscap lilies. —*Marsha Melder*
Shreveport, Louisiana

Black-capped chickadees can't resist my ponderosa pine. They split open the tree's pinecones and eat the inner seeds. —*Anne Fauvell*
Rapid City, South Dakota

Hummingbirds seem to prefer the nectar of my cypress vines. As soon as the vines start blooming, the birds ignore my sugar-water feeders and spend all their time at the flowers instead. —*Josephine Ayers*
Aiken, South Carolina

Large manicured lawns will not attract a large variety of birds. Instead, concentrate your efforts on planting trees and shrubs. They provide shelter to songbirds, protecting them from predators. Not many birds will feed far from a safe escape. I leave some of my grassy areas uncut for ground-nesting birds.

—*Frances Halliday*
Livonia, Michigan

Mourning doves often nest in my hanging potted plants. While I love the close-up view of these birds, I don't like that they ruin my plants. The solution? I created a nesting spot just for them.

I set up a 12-inch hanging basket in a secluded part of my yard and placed a small spider plant in it. The doves seem to appreciate the privacy and stay out of the other hanging baskets.

—*Nancy Zon*
Sunnyvale, California

A variety of plantings is one of the most important features of a bird-friendly backyard. Include conifers, deciduous trees (they lose their leaves) and fruit-bearing trees and shrubs. Also, plant seed and nectar-producing flowers in large clumps. The more there are in one area, the more birds they'll attract.

—*Darlene Polachic*
Saskatoon, Saskatchewan

Just like butterflies, hummingbirds flock to my zinnias and cosmos. Besides nectar, they feed on insects that are attracted to these blooms.

—*P. Tayor, Andalusia, Alabama*

Birds helped me start an interesting garden. They dropped several sunflower seeds in my yard, which sprouted into sunny surprises (above). Then I planted even more.

I purchased a 4-pound bag of mixed sunflower seeds, tossed them throughout my garden and let Mother Nature finish the job. Now my yard is full of sunflowers—and birds! —*Darlene Rokosky*
Thompson, Ohio

IT'S A FACT...
Dried gourds make terrific birdhouses. Seeds and instructions to grow them are available for $7 from the Purple Martin Conservation Association, Edinboro University of Pennsylvania, Edinboro PA 16444.

Chapter 7
Splish Splash

What's the one thing that will draw birds to your backyard like a magnet? Water!

Just as important as food, wild birds need water to drink and bathe. If you provide it, winged activity will surely follow.

But don't think a traditional birdbath is the only way to take the plunge. Readers have come up with all sorts of unique and easy ideas to create a perfect watering hole—from using recycled containers as makeshift baths to building elaborate backyard ponds.

Try some of these hints, and you're sure to make a big splash with the feathered friends in your neighborhood!

Photo: Maslowski Photo

Turn a leaky outdoor faucet into an effective birdbath dripper. I set a baking pan below the faucet and a large variety of birds quickly found the water source. *—Kelly Davis Prescott Valley, Arizona*

Birds were more interested in my birdbath after I moved it near a fence in my backyard. They land on a post, survey the yard, then hop to the bath. The fence provides a great spot for them to preen after they bathe, too. *—Betty Deaver Dell, Montana*

To provide a functional and attractive water source, I filled several square 12-inch hanging planters with potting soil. Then I nestled round saucers into the dirt and filled them with water. At each corner of the planter there's enough room to add a few small flowers. I use lobelia and pansies. *—Dave Gibler Portland, Oregon*

Use a large plastic trough, like those used for mixing cement, to make a small pond. It works great. Mine's about 24 x 36 inches and 10 inches deep.

Just bury the trough to ground level, hide the edge with flat stones and place flowers around it. Rocks in the middle of the pond help birds drink and bathe. *—Charlotte Clark Glenpool, Oklahoma*

IT'S A FACT...

One of the biggest favors you can do for birds in winter is offer a heated water supply.

My husband and I enhanced our backyard pond by placing white Christmas lights among the surrounding rocks. It's beautiful when the sun is setting. The birds like to visit in the early evening when the lights come on. *—Jean Shpock Freeland, Pennsylvania*

We don't own our property, so we couldn't install a regular in-ground pond to attract birds. So we settled for a smaller above-ground pond, instead (above).

We lined two half oak barrels with black plastic and filled them with water, plants, fish and snails. The plants hide the hoses from a circulating pump that moves water between the two barrels. Place cinder blocks or stacked bricks in the pond so the birds have a safe place to perch.

Not only does our little pond provide the sounds of a mini waterfall, it attracts many birds as well. *—Dana Kayal Campbell River, British Columbia*

Jim Sibilski

Add a birdbath dripper to attract more winged activity to your backyard. Birds flock to the moving water and the sound it makes. I made mine out of these common items you'll find at the hardware store:

- Outdoor water spigot fit with a Y-connector with shut-offs.
- Garden hose.
- 1/2-inch female brass clinch coupling.
- 1 foot of 5/16-inch (inside diameter) plastic tubing.
- About 5 feet of 5/16-inch copper tubing (length will vary with the size of the birdbath).
- Two plastic cable ties, long enough to wrap around the birdbath pedestal.
- Epoxy glue.
- Coffee can.

Attach the garden hose to the Y-connector at the spigot, extending the hose to the birdbath.

Set aside. At the birdbath, insert the plastic tubing into the 1/2-inch end of the coupling and push it through so about 1 inch extends past the coupling. Apply a thin layer of epoxy to this end and pull it back into the coupling so it's flush inside, creating a seal.

Carefully bend one end of the copper tubing around the coffee can to form a candy-cane shape (see illustration above). Continue curving it down the side of your birdbath to the base. Cut off what remains. Then secure the tubing to the birdbath pedestal with cable ties.

Insert the straight end of the copper tubing into the plastic tube. Connect the coupling to your garden hose. Adjust the spigot and shut-off, so water slowly drips into your birdbath.

—Cliff Muehlenberg
Pewaukee, Wisconsin

I've found an easy and inexpensive way to make my own birdbaths (above). I nestle terra-cotta-colored plastic drainage trays—the kind used under potted plants—in the rings of a tomato cage. I cut three notches in the rim of the bottom tray so it will fit around the wire legs. The legs can be anchored in the ground to make the birdbath stable before I fill it with fresh water.

—*Sue Myers, East Troy, Wisconsin*

When the plant we placed near our birdbath died, the tomato cage that supported it became a convenient perch for the birds. They use it to wait in line for the bath or for a place to preen afterward. Sometimes we see several birds perched on each rung. —*Marilyn Lenart*
St. Clair Beach, Ontario

Our old satellite dish makes an economical birdbath. I buried it so the rim was level with the ground, placed small rocks around the edges and filled it with water. Because it's only a few inches deep, there was no need to place additional rocks for birds to perch on. —*Elliot Mullet*
Nashwauk, Minnesota

To prevent messy buildup in our birdbaths, we fill a bucket with tap water and let it sit for a few days before adding it to the baths. We're not sure why, but this seems to slow the growth of algae.

—*Charley and Judy Sayre*
Newark, Ohio

Since we installed a heater to our small backyard pond, our yard is a hub of winter avian activity. Our goldfish survive year-round, and birds and other wildlife always have a place to drink and bathe.

—*Cheryl Wofford, Pekin, Illinois*

Place a terra-cotta saucer on a flowerpot and you'll create a simple and effective birdbath (above). It's shallow enough for birds to wade in the water and large enough to accommodate several at once.

—*Sheryl Neal, Carrollton, Ohio*

Many birdbaths get dirty or quickly dry out unless you can clean them on a daily basis. So I decided to create a "bird pool" (above) in my backyard that would fill itself.

I dug a small 12- x 18-inch hole that's about 2 inches deep. Then I lined it with a thin layer of premixed concrete and hired a plumber to install a water pipe with a faucet right next to it. Not only does the dripping water keep it constantly replenished, but the sound helps attract more birds. —*Hugh Smith*
Solvang, California

To provide plenty of water for small backyard birds, I use two watering dishes designed for baby chickens. The waterers attach to quart-sized canning jars, which I fill with fresh water daily. Butterflies like them, too. —*Cecilia Mergen*
Colman, South Dakota

In summer, I often spray water on my trees and shrubs, which keeps them healthy and also attracts winged wildlife. The mist from my hose invites hummingbirds and butterflies, while the water dripping from leaves seems to satisfy thirsty birds for hours. —*Glenda Jordan*
Austell, Georgia

Birds were bathing in my rain barrels, but some couldn't get out. So I lined the inside of the barrel with hardware cloth, giving them something to cling to. —*Inge Genoe*
Coopersburg, Pennsylvania

IT'S A FACT...
Most birds prefer a water depth of only 1 to 3 inches. If your birdbath is deeper, add some flat stones.

Here's how I made a birdbath for less than $5. I dug a shallow birdbath-shaped depression in a pile of loose dirt and covered it with a plastic tarp. Then I made a batch of premixed cement in a wheelbarrow and poured it into the tarp to form a shallow basin with a rim about 1-1/2 inches thick. The final touch was a rock in the center (see photo above).

After about 3 days, the cement firmly set. I removed the birdbath and placed it on a pile of large stones in a safe spot in my yard.

—*Richard Goerg, Bruce, Alberta*

The winters are quite cold here in Canada, so I wanted to provide a heated birdbath for feathered friends. My husband, Ed, came up with this solution:

He built a small wooden box—much like a birdhouse—with a roof and a roomy entrance for the birds. Then we inserted a spotlight through the bottom and placed a metal hubcap on it. The light produces enough heat so the water in the hubcap doesn't freeze.

Plenty of birds come to drink from this reliable water source, and a pair of mourning doves even bathed in it! —*Lynne Hurlburt Welland, Ontario*

IT'S A FACT...

Follow these birdbath tips from the Cornell Lab of Ornithology, Ithaca, New York, and your backyard will be the most popular watering hole in the neighborhood:

• Look for a basin that can be easily cleaned and has a gentle slope so birds can wade into the water.

• In winter, use heavy-duty plastic birdbaths. They're less likely to break if the water freezes.

• When temperatures fall below freezing, use a birdbath heater to provide a constant source of water.

• Try to make the birdbath resemble a natural puddle by positioning it close to the ground.

• Birds can't fly well when they're wet. Place birdbaths near shrubs and trees in case they need to escape from predators.

• Clean your birdbath every couple of days.

ASK GEORGE

Help! I've had two white plastic birdbaths in my yard for years and have never seen a bird use them. I've changed locations as well as put a few flat rocks in them for birds to perch on. What am I doing wrong?
—Shelia Saxton
Gallipolis Ferry, West Virginia

George: Try locating the birdbaths closer to a shrub, tree or other natural cover that will provide an escape for the birds should they feel threatened. Also, the water may be difficult for your feathered friends to see in the white baths. By painting them an earth color, the water might be more visible.

Birds don't need an elaborate bath—they appreciate smaller basins as well. I place shallow dishes of water throughout my yard, making sure the water isn't deeper than 1-1/2 inches. Although I need to change the water every day to keep them clean, I can host lots of winged bathers at once.
—*Marlene Condon, Crozet, Virginia*

My birdbath sits below a beautiful wisteria tree. Its provides shade to keep the water cool and serves as nearby protective cover for the birds that use it. Plus, the tree's dangling blooms smell wonderful!
—*Carolyn Covey*
San Bernardino, California

I make sure my birdbaths are kept full in spring because many birds, like Steller's jays and barn swallows, need water to create mud for their nests. —*Clara Belle Tye*
Washougal, Washington

Here in the desert, it's difficult to keep my birdbath full. To solve the problem, I purchased a small mister that connects directly to my garden hose. The spray of water slowly replenishes the water that has evaporated. —*Edith Osborn*
Phoenix, Arizona

Our birdbath "complex"—a system of backyard ponds that flow from one to another—is the perfect addition to our backyard. We've spotted at least 38 different species of birds drinking or bathing in the ponds. —*Larry O'Neal*
Rockford, Illinois

When searching rummage sales and flea markets, I look for sturdy antique table legs. They make unique birdbath pedestals. Then I use an old sink or pan as a basin, attaching them with silicon caulk or a bolt and rubber washer.
—*Dan Miller, Longmont, Colorado*

European starlings are such messy bathers that they often splash all the water out of my birdbath, especially in winter. Then I have to venture into the cold and snow to refill the bath—often several times a day. So I came up with this effective solution:

I placed lightweight plastic garden fencing over the birdbath and keep it in place by setting a few small stones on it (above). The fencing has large holes so birds can still access the water. But now only a couple of birds can bathe at a time, reducing the amount of water spilled over the edge. —*Mary Clay Colorado Springs, Colorado*

Water attracts more birds to my yard than feeders do. So I provide numerous water dishes and birdbaths and have attracted doves, woodpeckers, mallards, great blue herons, snowy egrets and great egrets.

—*Lou Kelley, Tampa, Florida*

For an economical ground-level birdbath, begin with a child's snow saucer. Coat the inside with waterproof adhesive and spread a large bag of pea-sized aquarium gravel on it. Allow the glue to dry for several days, then nestle the bath in your garden. Place a couple larger rocks in the center and fill it with water.

—*Jacqueline Wassmuth Moberly, Missouri*

When it comes to finding a place to bathe, birds aren't picky—a simple puddle on the ground will do just fine.

You can easily "create" a puddle by overturning a garbage can lid and filling it with water.

—*Jenny Butenhoff Franklin, Wisconsin*

I connected my birdbath heater to an outdoor timer. It comes on each morning to thaw the ice that formed overnight. —*Chuck Straub Barrie, Ontario*

IT'S A FACT...

After a bird is finished bathing, it flies to a nearby perch to comb its feathers with its bill. This is called preening, a process that removes dirt and parasites, while realigning the barbs of its feathers so they lock together.

Maintaining healthy feathers is vital to a bird's survival. Proper conditioning helps them quickly escape predators and offers protection from the elements.

To create a fresh backyard water source, use a small needle to poke a hole in the bottom of a 1-gallon juice container, preferably one with a plastic handle. Fill the container with water and hang it from a tree or shepherd's hook, making sure the lid is loose so air can enter the bottle and allow water to drip. For an informal birdbath, place a large flowerpot saucer below the dripping water.
— *Nancy Draheim*
Delta, Ohio

To keep water from freezing in winter, I place it in a large black rubber pan that's designed to feed horses. The dark color absorbs the sun's rays and retains heat, so I rarely have to worry about it freezing over.

When temperatures are really cold, I pour hot water in the dish in the morning and again at night. And because the pan is pliable, if ice does form, I simply twist it to pop out the ice out.
— *Phyllis Hubbard*
Corydon, Indiana

Raccoons dumped my plastic birdbath night after night, so I replaced the wobbly pedestal with a trash can. I set the basin in the plastic can (it fit perfectly in a 20-gallon container) and filled it with water.

The raccoons still visit the bath, but they haven't tipped it.
— *Patricia Condelli*
New Kensington, Pennsylvania

Use a tomato cage to keep crows out of your birdbath. Just cut off the legs and place it upside down in the basin.
— *Marion Lewis*
Normandy Park, Washington

My husband, Ray, and I built a "water world" in our backyard. We used rocks to create a pond with a beautiful waterfall and planted plenty of flowers around it. We especially enjoyed watching a pair of blue jays raise a family in our little oasis. It was amazing to watch the young birds take their first dip in the refreshing water.
— *Sue Rager*
Leesburg, Florida

Most birds prefer shallow water. So we modified our deep bath by placing rocks and stones in the bottom so birds of all sizes can comfortably drink or bathe.
— *Bob and June Kibler*
Middletown, Ohio

A fountain kit for a half-barrel works well (without the barrel) as a small pond in our backyard (above). It was more affordable than the rigid plastic ponds and had everything I needed—a flexible plastic liner, a pump and fountain nozzles.

I simply dug a shallow hole 4 feet in diameter and lined it with the heavy plastic. Then I placed the fountain in the middle, spread some aquarium gravel on the bottom and filled the pond with water. To help it blend in with the landscape, I added some pretty rocks and plants around the water's edge. The birds love stopping to bathe and drink from it.
—*Helynn Schufletowski*
Humbird, Wisconsin

For a low-cost and portable bird-bath, I used metal flowerpot stand—the kind that sticks in the ground like a stake—and top it with a glass pie plate. It was simple to set up and even easier to clean. I just take the pie plate inside and wash it in the sink or dishwasher. —*Dee Fannin*
Santa Rosa, California

I turned an ordinary frying pan into a simple birdbath. I set it in thick patch of pampas grass to provide protective cover. The birds flock to it. —*Lydia Post*
Parchment, Michigan

ASK GEORGE
I read that heated birdbaths are bad for birds because their wet feet then stick when they land on a cold branch. Is this fact or fiction? —*Rhonda Fetters*
Grayling, Michigan

George: There's no evidence that heated birdbaths are bad for birds. Birds' legs receive little blood circulation and are covered with horny scales. As a result, their feet are nearly impervious to severe cold temperatures. Besides, during very cold weather, birds are more apt to drink than bathe at birdbaths.

Fill it with water and add containers of Japanese irises, as well as small water lilies and floating water hyacinths.

One morning, I watched a pair of Steller's jays return to my makeshift pond again and again to collect mud for their nests. —*Clara Belle Tye*
Washougal, Washington

I scour rummage sales for items that can be used as birdbaths. My favorite discoveries are Chinese woks. They make perfect makeshift baths for ground-feeding birds.
—*Gloria Meredith*
Harrington, Delaware

When summer's heat quickly evaporates the water in my birdbaths, I set out a child's rigid plastic wading pool, fill the bottom with sand and rocks, set a couple water-tolerant plants in it and fill it with a couple inches of water. Every animal—from birds to squirrels—enjoys this oasis during the hot dry days. —*Jean Mitchell*
Plant City, Florida

We help birds beat the summer heat with this simple technique. I fill a 1-gallon milk jug with water, freeze it overnight and put it upside down on our deck railing in the morning. Water slowly drips into a dish below as the ice melts.

We made a decorative house (above) to disguise the jug, but the birds aren't picky about how you present it. —*Tom and Gwen Phillips*
Denver, New York

For an easy and effective water garden, use a child's wading pool.

There was little activity at my birdbath, until I exchanged my white basin for a terra cotta one. Almost immediately after I made the switch, birds began stopping by to drink. —*Angela Martinez*
Clifton, Colorado

In summer we fill our birdbaths with water that drips from our air conditioner. Using this distilled water helps reduce algae.
—*Charley and Judy Sayre*
Newark, Ohio

We used a pump to create a lovely shower for the birds (above). Water drips from a metal watering can into the bath and an ivy-covered hose carries it back up to the can. The birds flock to this constant flow of water.   —*Peggy Sabine*
East Hampton, Massachusetts

Old frying pans can be easily converted into birdbaths. Just remove the handles (be sure to file down or cover any sharp edges). Then dig holes 18 inches deep (you may need to go deeper if frost is a problem) with a post-hole digger and sink 4-foot pressure-treated fence posts into the ground—one to support each recycled pan. To secure them to the posts, predrill a 1/4-inch hole in the center of each pan. For a tight seal, use rubber washers or waterproof caulk around the hole as you attach it with screws.
—*Jo Morton*
Satellite Beach, Florida

If you ever collected seashells, you probably have some extras stored someplace waiting for a good idea. We'll here's one. Just place them around the edges of your water garden. We've been amused to see small frogs perching in our shells. We've also seen birds, butterflies, moths and dragonflies drinking from rainwater collected in them.
—*Lynne McLernon*
Lake Geneva, Wisconsin

I line my birdbath with aluminum foil and place a rock on the foil to hold it in place. After about a week, I replace the foil. It's a no-scrub way to keep my birdbath clean.
—*Larry Vink, Topeka, Kansas*

A heated dog dish makes a great winter birdbath. Just fill one with water and set it near your feeders.
—*Geraldine Grisdale*
Mt. Pleasant, Michigan

Water is an important resource for birds, but too much water can be dangerous. One day I came home from work and found four baby birds that perished in my fishpond. We finally found a way to prevent this. We now cover our pond with a screen that's just below the surface of the water. Birds can safely bathe and drink, but they also have a safe way to climb out.   —*Norma Hemstreet*
Enumclaw, Washington

By George… Since moving water makes birdbaths even more attractive to birds, such as finches, warblers and grosbeaks, try adding a mister, a dripper or a fountain to the birdbath. —*George Harrison Contributing Editor*

If you don't have room for a pond, try using a standard washtub. Mine measures only 20 by 24 inches but still lets me enjoy the simple pleasures of a water garden. I set it in the ground and used a small pump to create a waterfall that cascades down over stones and into the pond. It's a favorite stop for birds in the area. —*Nancy Singer Quakertown, Pennsylvania*

Texas summers are hot, so I devised a way to provide cool water for my birds. Each night, I freeze containers of water in empty waxed milk cartons. When I come home for lunch, I put one of the blocks of ice in the birdbath. It doesn't take long for the birds to find the cool water. I add another block when I return home in the evening. —*Erma Short Texarkana, Texas*

Our birdbath is very low maintenance. It's a 12-inch flowerpot tray with three holes drilled in the rim, so we could tie string to it and suspend the bath from a shepherd's hook. Although the birds don't often bathe in it, they frequently stop by for a quick drink. —*O.J. and Jean Sergent Charlevoix, Michigan*

To make refilling a breeze in winter, we set our heated birdbath right outside a window (below). Now we just have to slide it open to add water—no more bundling up! —*Jeannine Fitzgeralds Aurora, Colorado*

IT'S A FACT…
Most birds drink by using their bills to scoop up water, then tip their heads back to swallow.

My daughter, Rebecca Brinkman, has created many interesting and unusual woodworking projects, but her birdbath (above) is the conversation piece in her Thornton, Colorado backyard.

The actual bath is a saucer from a large plastic flowerpot. To hold it, she crafted an adjustable childlike wood figure that hangs upside down from a horizontal pole. She anchored the legs with bolts to keep it from swinging in the wind. It definitely adds a bit of whimsical fun to the backyard.   —*Dorothy Richards*
Kansas City, Missouri

I place large colorful marbles in my birdbaths. They seem to attract more winged activity.   —*Deane Taylor*
Summerfield, North Carolina

My birdbath refills itself. I set a large dish below a downspout. Even a little rain means the birdbath is filled without any extra effort.
—*Candi Schopfer, Chauvin, Alberta*

I use a new oil pan purchased from my local automotive store as a birdbath. A rock holds it in place. The birds seem to enjoy sitting on the rock as they wait their turn to bathe.
—*Verna Olson*
Fargo, North Dakota

I moved a cross section of a tree trunk to my garden and put a birdbath basin on top of it (below). Now that I've planted flowers around the stump, I often see birds putting it to use. One day, five American robins frolicked in the water at the same time.   —*Virginia Askew*
Opelika, Alabama

Attract birds to your bath with the sound of water. A simple way to do this is by making a tiny hole in the bottom of a plastic bucket. Fill the bucket with water and insert a nail or bent paper clip into the hole. Place the bucket over a birdbath, and let it slowly drip. You'll be surprised how many birds will take notice.
—*Elinor Wellhausen, Kirtland, Ohio*

Many people place rocks in their birdbaths to provide perches, but I use them for another purpose. During the cold Colorado winters, the water surrounding the rocks does not freeze. So birds have a constant water supply, even when the temperature drops.   —*Frank Portman Colorado Springs, Colorado*

Instead of bringing fish from our backyard pond inside for winter, I cover the pond with an A-frame made of clear plastic and treated wood. When the temperature drops to 15°, I turn on the recirculating pump. The moving water and greenhouse keep the water from freezing, even when the temperature gets down to –30°.   —*Steven Simpson Pleasantville, Iowa*

It's important to keep fresh water available, even in winter. But it's sometimes difficult to remove the ice that forms in our birdbaths. Instead, we make sure the water in our small garden pond doesn't freeze over. Each morning I break a hole in the ice with a hammer. Then the birds have access to the water all day.   —*Clara Belle Tye Washougal, Washington*

To protect our cement birdbath from cracking in winter, we bring it indoors. In its place, we stack three 5-gallon plastic buckets, weighing them down with a couple of bricks, then put an upside-down trash can lid on top (above). We use another brick to hold the lid in place and fill it with water. It doesn't look as nice as our beautiful formal bath, but it works just as well!
—*Bruce and Connie Smith Sunbury, Pennsylvania*

Hang a garden hose from a tree limb above your birdbath. I let mine *slowly* drip. The birds line up once they hear the sound.   —*Joan Allen Aiken, South Carolina*

When constructing a pond for your backyard, make sure to include an area where the water is less than 2-1/2 inches deep, so the birds can safely bathe and drink from it.
—*Nora Blose Enka, North Carolina*

We love squirrels as much as the birds, so we offer them a water source of their own. We set up a separate birdbath, and my husband, David, built a tiny ladder for them to scurry up to the water hole. The furry acrobats figured out this was a "squirrel bath" in no time! —*Joy Walters, Toulon, Illinois*

from freezing, even when the temperature reaches 20°. —*Betty Winston Asheville, North Carolina*

Since my husband ran a water line from our house to the birdbath, I never have to refill it. He installed a faucet on the end that slowly drips into the bath. And to disguise the pipe, I planted some ivy at its base.
—*Jean Wallace Gulf Shores, Alabama*

Our six birdbaths are functional and beautiful in winter since we equipped them with light bulbs. We installed 40-watt bulbs inside the white plastic pedestals, which now emit a lovely glow at night.

We leave the lights on all day to keep the water from freezing. In summer, I use 15-watt bulbs to cast a warm glow throughout my gardens in the evening. —*Sylvia Marker Boise, Idaho*

Use an old slow cooker as a winter birdbath. At a low setting, water will not freeze. I set a piece of lattice across the top of mine, so birds can sit on it while they drink.
—*Audrey Samplawski Chetek, Wisconsin*

Solar energy keeps my birdbath from freezing. I painted it black and keep it in a sunny location. It absorbs the sun's rays and prevents the water

On cold mornings, my sister, Angie, heats a teapot of water and pours it into her birdbath (below). The hot water thaws the ice that formed overnight and keeps it from freezing all day.
—*Joe De Calabash, North Carolina*

Chapter 8
Squeaky Clean

Most backyard bird-watchers know it's important to keep bird feeders, birdbaths and nest boxes clean for their feathered friends. It's just part of maintaining a healthy bird habitat.

But that doesn't mean it has to be a chore. In fact, many readers have devised some pretty inventive ways to make cleanup a snap.

That way, you can spend less time scrubbing and more time enjoying the avian activity that flocks to your tidy yard.

I purchased a grill brush to keep my birdbath looking clean. Its wire bristles are strong enough to break up the most stubborn grime.

—*Barbara Simpson*
Blue Mountain, Mississippi

Hummingbirds don't like to wait for their food while I wash their sugar-water feeder, so I hang a spare one while I'm busy cleaning.

—*Judy Talbott, Rochester, Indiana*

I had trouble cleaning our large cedar bird feeder because it would not fit in our sink. My husband suggested I take it to a self-serve car wash. The high-pressure washer did the trick. It removed every trace of seed and dirt without any hassle.

—*Sheryl Miller*
Fogo, Newfoundland

Here is an easy way to make your birdbath sparkle. Toss a handful of sand into the basin and scrub it with a clean brush. The grit helps grind away any residue.

—*Marilyn Clancy*
Englewood, Florida

Instead of using harsh soaps to clean my sugar-water feeders, I fill them with water, add 2 to 3 tablespoons of fine gravel and shake them until the residue is gone. It usually takes just a minute or two.

—*Anna Davis, Warsaw, Ohio*

Washing birdbaths can be a chore, but I found a way to get the job done in a snap. I place a piece of sturdy black weed barrier in the bottom of the birdbath before filling it. When the basin gets dirty, I simply lift the material out, shake it clean, hose it off and put it back in the birdbath. There's no need to scrub!

—*Brad Walsh*
Lee's Summit, Missouri

Clean hummingbird feeders in a solution of 1/4 cup bleach and 3/4 cup water. I put an old necklace chain in the feeder and vigorously shake it. After thoroughly rinsing several times, the feeder is ready to use.

—*Vernell Krueger*
Campbellsport, Wisconsin

I clean my birdhouses in fall, then store them inside all winter. That way, mice don't nest in them.

—*Arthur Stefanelli*
Fairview, Pennsylvania

I use a watering can (above) to make filling my feeders a breeze. Just remove the head from the spout and pour it in. It works great for filling small feeders.

—*Carl Correll*
Munfordville, Kentucky

My birdbaths get cleaned at night while I sleep. I fill the basins with water and add 2 ounces of household bleach. Then I cover them with trash-can lids to keep critters out. In the morning, I remove the lids, thoroughly rinse the baths and refill with water. —*Earl Ratz*
Stratford, Ontario

An old toothbrush is my secret weapon for cleaning sugar-water feeders. It's great for getting into the small feeding ports.
—*Mrs. David Ross*
Henderson, Tennessee

I could never get my hummingbird feeders completely clean, until I discovered this method. Place a few uncooked navy beans in the feeder with some water and gently shake. Even the hard-to-reach crevices come clean. —*Lynn Ray*
Greenup, Illinois

Since I replaced the bottom of my birdhouse with a sliding board, cleaning is easy. I simply remove the board and the house's contents fall to the ground. —*Della Johnson*
Bellingham, Washington

Don't throw away used pieces of heavy-duty aluminum foil. Crumple them to use as birdbath scrubbers. They work similar to scouring pads and don't cost a thing. I've found old mesh onion bags work well, too.
—*Lois Nietert*
McMurray, Pennsylvania

Soak hummingbird feeders in a bucket of 1 cup bleach and 2 gal-

I learned it's sometimes best to leave birdhouse cleaning until early spring. Birds and other small animals may use the old nesting material to keep warm on cold winter nights.

When cleaning the birdhouse, remove all debris and sterilize the house by pouring boiling water through it. Make any necessary repairs before rehanging.
—*Judy Singh*
Maryville, Tennessee

lons of water. I let them sit for 20 to 30 minutes and then thoroughly rinse. I like this approach because no scrubbing is needed. —*Lois Mullen*
Alice, Texas

My concrete birdbath sparkles after I scour it with Ajax kitchen cleaner. I use a good scrub brush then rinse the basin thoroughly before refilling. —*Hildegard Mengot*
Mount Pleasant, Michigan

109

Cut the bottom off a plastic 2- or 3-liter soft drink bottle and leave the cap on to create a handy birdseed scoop. When you're ready to fill your feeders, just remove the cap, and the seed conveniently funnels through the bottle's spout.
—*Carol Smith*
Tecumseh, Oklahoma

Place a few pennies in your birdbath. They slow down algae buildup. —*Patty Lowney*
Appleton, Wisconsin

I use an old-fashioned percolator brush to clean my hummingbird feeders. —*Fern Brown*
Clayton, Indiana

Baby bottle brushes are perfect for scrubbing hummingbird feeders. The bristles are small enough to reach into the tiny crevices and strong enough to scrub away tough grime. —*Tabatha Arden*
Madisonville, Tennessee

Seed is constantly spilling from our tray feeder onto the ground. It kills the grass and wastes seed. So we built a base of patio bricks below the feeder (left). Not only does it catch the spills, it provides a second feeding area for birds on the ground.
—*Barry and Hanna Phillips*
Waco, Texas

ASK GEORGE
What's the best way to clean sugar-water feeders? I have a tough time getting rid of the sticky residue. —*Donald Kraus Erie, Pennsylvania*

George: Soap and hot water, and perhaps a little vinegar, will do a good job getting your hummingbird feeders squeaky clean. Use a tiny bottle brush or pipe cleaner to scrub off the sticky residue in the feeding ports.

It's best to clean the feeder often—about once every week or two.

A new toilet brush is the perfect tool to keep birdbaths sparkling clean. A couple times a week I scrub the bath, rinse it out and refill with clean water. —*Bradlee Maxwell Washington Court House, Ohio*

I found a way to fill my tube feeders without spilling seed. I use a funnel that's designed for home canning. It's slightly smaller than the

tube feeder's opening so it fits perfectly. No more mess!
—Carol Palumbo
Williamsville, New York

When my wife's parents moved off their dairy farm, I saved some of their old metal milk cans for storing different types of birdseed. They keep the seed dry, are critter resistant and are quite decorative. My sister-in-law painted wildlife scenes on them. *—Dave Zueger*
Fargo, North Dakota

I keep my nectar feeders clean by placing a small piece of netting in the feeder. Just swish it around with some water, and the netting cleans out the residue. *—Pat Willborn*
Huntsville, Texas

To prevent fallen seed from germinating below my bird feeder, I placed a large plastic circular mat below it. The mat is designed to keep grass from growing under fruit trees, so it's a perfect fit. When it's time to tidy up the feeding area, I just remove the mat, shake and wash it off. *—Bev Dennison*
Crandon, Wisconsin

When I purchase a new bird feeder, I always get two. That way, when the first feeder gets dirty, I can take it down, replace it with the spare one and clean the original when I have a little extra time.
—Kathleen Ryan
Oklahoma City, Oklahoma

Some of my birdhouses don't have access doors for cleaning. So I use a fishhook remover to break up old nests. Tilt the house so the nesting material falls toward the entrance hole. Then just simply shake it out. *—Pat Daly*
Waterford, Ontario

My husband discovered a way to avoid the tedious scrubbing usually needed to clean birdbaths. He painted several coats of clear exterior polyurethane inside the basin. Now we can wipe the grime away with a rag. *—Lori Paulson*
Silver Cliff, Wisconsin

I store my birdseed in large popcorn tins—the kind that are popular around the holidays. The colorful tins hold a lot of seed, are easy to handle and keep critters out.
—Ruby Houchen
Citrus Heights, California

To keep squirrels and woodpeckers from remodeling my birdhouse entrance, I attached a metal wall plate for a 220 electrical outlet over the hole (right). The 1-3/8-inch hole is just right for many species of birds and "home wreckers" aren't able to chew through it.

—Diane Larkin
Churchville, Pennsylvania

ASK GEORGE

Is there a way to keep birdseed from sprouting? I feed a lot of birds by scattering seed on the ground, but the sprouts have become a real problem.
—*Sharon Severs*
San Jose, California

George: Some birdseed, such as niger (thistle), is sterilized and shouldn't sprout. Others, including sunflower seed, are not.

I only know one safe way to keep birdseed from sprouting—present it to the birds in a tray with sides. That should prevent most spillage and will help solve your problem.

To keep my sugar-water feeder clean, I put an old beaded necklace in it, fill it with water and shake. The beads scrub the surface clean.
—*Jo Ann Sheldon*
Arkansas City, Kansas

My husband discovered car wash soap works great for cleaning our birdbaths. After applying the soap, he scrubs the surface with a stiff brush and the dirt comes right off. Then he rinses it several times before filling it with fresh water.
—*Connie Dietrich*
Lambertville, Michigan

Wrap a damp cotton ball around a barbecue skewer to clean sugar-water feeders. I use a little bit of mild soap, too, and thoroughly rinse.
—*Anna Victoria Reich*
Albuquerque, New Mexico

A power washer makes the time-consuming task of cleaning bird feeders much easier. My small portable power washer loosens all the debris. Then I fill a spray bottle

with a mixture of 1/8 cup bleach and 1 cup water and spray the entire feeder. After about 5 minutes, I thoroughly rinse the feeder with the power washer again and place it in a sunny spot to dry completely before I refill it.
—*Debbie Snook*
Eugene, Oregon

The easiest way to clean a birdhouse is by first soaking the inside with water. I use a spray bottle, then scrape out the old nesting materials. I wear a mask to cover my mouth and nose so I don't inhale any debris.
—*Tom Kovach*
Park Rapids, Minnesota

When it's time to wash my birdbath, I empty the water, pour baking soda into the basin and scrub it with a paper towel. I've found this method cleans even the dirtiest baths.
—*Michelle Loomis*
Oswego, New York

Keeping my heavy cement birdbath clean was just too difficult, so I set a clay flowerpot saucer of a slightly smaller circumference in the basin. Now I just empty the dirty water from the dish and carry it to the sink to clean it out. Our birds have clean water all summer.
—*Dolores Renner*
Leonardville, Kansas

Our cement birdbath is heavy, making it difficult to empty and clean. To solve the problem, we drilled a hole in the bottom of the basin and used a bathtub stopper to plug it up. When it's time to drain the water for cleaning, we simply "pull the plug". —*Shirley Mazzini*
Lodi, California

My nectar feeders sparkle after I submerge them in a bucket filled with warm water and a couple denture-cleaning tablets. I let the feeders soak for about 5 minutes, then rinse them thoroughly with warm water until all the suds are gone.
—*Patricia Craig*
Harbor Springs, Michigan

To clean my thistle feeders thoroughly, I fill a bucket with warm water and submerge the feeder in it. I then use a toothbrush with some baking soda to scrub away dirt and grime. —*Margy Calvin*
El Centro, California

I found the perfect tool for scrubbing dirty hummingbird feeder ports—a mascara brush. Just clean the tiny wand with warm soapy water until there's no trace of mascara on it. —*Judy Talbott*
Rochester, Indiana

My birdbath basin (above) is glazed ceramic, which means it has a smooth shiny surface. This makes it easier to clean than other birdbaths. I just spray it with a little water to remove the algae and dirt. The birds love it, too! —*Karen Denton*
Nipomo, California

For an algae-free birdbath, squeeze a few drops of dark food coloring into the water. The sun can't penetrate the darker colored water, so algae doesn't grow.
—*Rhonda Mech*
Crivitz, Wisconsin

To keep my three ponds clean, I put washable furnace filters in the waterfall. I take the filters out every 2 weeks and wash them.

—*Rita Redman*
Kennett, Missouri

Our heavy concrete birdbath was nearly impossible to clean, until I discovered a simple remedy. I set a glass pie dish inside it. Since it's clear, it doesn't detract from the bath's beauty. Plus it's simple to clean. I just take out the dish and place it in the dishwasher.

—*Dee Fannin*
Santa Rosa, California

Cleaning up spilled birdseed is a difficult task because I have trouble bending. But I came up with a simple solution. I put the feeder post through the umbrella hole of an unused picnic table. Now the table catches most of the seed that would have landed on the ground. It's a breeze to clean off…and no bending!

—*Darlene Price*
Roswell, Georgia

I use a rust-resistant soap pad to keep my concrete birdbath clean. It helps me quickly remove water stains and algae buildup. When I'm done, I make sure to rinse the bath thoroughly.

—*Mabel Heselton*
West Plains, Missouri

Since I put three snails in my birdbath, it no longer turns green from algae. The snails take care of cleaning it for me…and I sure don't miss the scrubbing. —*Evelyn Mack*
Green Bay, Wisconsin

After washing my thistle tube feeders, I dry them with a hair dryer. It blows the remaining water right out of the feeder ports. It's much easier and more effective than using a towel. —*Arene Holt*
Vancouver, British Columbia

A male northern cardinal started to attack its reflection in our vehicle's side mirrors (below), and the scratches and dirt it left behind quickly became a nuisance. So we came up with a clever and simple solution—covering the mirrors with

plastic grocery bags. All we do is tie the bags in place whenever we park the car. —*Cindy Heimbach*
Fleetwood, Pennsylvania

Our morning newspaper is delivered in a narrow plastic bag. Instead of tossing the bags, I use them when I clean and refill our suet

By George... To keep algae from overtaking my birdbaths, I use household bleach.

Several times a summer, I drain the baths, pour pure bleach on all the surfaces and let it sit or scrub it a little. Then I rinse the baths thoroughly with fresh water, three or four times, before refilling them with more fresh water.

Just make sure to keep the birdbath covered with a garbage can lid or in a place that birds can't reach while the bleach does its work.

—George Harrison
Contributing Editor

cages. The bags fit perfectly over my hands and keep them from getting greasy.
—Art Richter
Woodstock, Illinois

Dishwasher granules are the perfect cleanser for my hummingbird feeders. I add 1 teaspoon of the soap to the feeder with some hot water. As I shake the feeder, the mixture scrubs away the residue. I rinse until no bubbles remain.
—Sally Canniff
Randolph, New York

I read about this English remedy for birdbath algae. After filling a clean birdbath with fresh water, place a bundle of six to eight stems of lavender in the water. One bundle will keep the water algae-free for 2 or 3 weeks.

I've used this method for months and haven't seen algae in my birdbath since!
—Mary Huiatt
Beckley, West Virginia

It's important to keep hummingbird feeders clean and filled with fresh sugar water. The sweet solution quickly spoils in warm weather. I wash my feeders with hot water and refill them every 2 to 3 days.
—Alice Pfister
Simi Valley, California

If I notice bugs in a container of birdseed, I place it in the freezer for 48 hours. It seems to keep the little pests under control.
—Martha Goodfellow
Brush Prairie, Washington

I keep seed from landing on my lawn by placing a carpet scrap below the feeder (at right). I got the remnant free from a local carpet store. I just cut a 2-inch slit in the piece of carpeting and slid it around the pole.
—Joan Rousseau
Dudley,
Massachusetts

It's often difficult to get my hands completely clean after maintaining a bird-friendly yard. But I've found a surefire solution. I dissolve a denture-cleaning tablet in warm water and soak my hands for a couple of minutes. It leaves them clean and soft. *—Donna Michels* *Green Rock, Illinois*

To keep our bird feeders clean, I fill my dishwasher with their "dirty dishes" once a week. I rinse the feeders with a hose first, so seed doesn't clog the dishwasher. Then I run them through normal washing cycle. *—Annette MacDonald* *Hampton, Ontario*

Provide nesting material in a suet cage. This keeps the lightweight material, such as tissue and yarn, from blowing around your backyard. *—Gloria Ashbaugh* *Lynchburg, Tennessee*

I offer suet to my backyard birds in old mesh onion bags. When the food is gone, I throw the bags away. It's much easier than trying to wash greasy suet cages. *—Penny Bailey* *Maple Plain, Minnesota*

I use a toothbrush to keep my bird feeders super clean. *—Terry Maiorana* *Ashford, Connecticut*

Wash your feeders periodically to reduce the spread of disease among your avian friends. I make my own disinfecting solution by mixing 2 ounces of bleach to 1 gallon of water.

Use bottle brushes and pot scrubbers (the long-handled brush type) to help clean in the tight areas. Then rinse thoroughly and set the bird feeders in the sun to dry. *—Roland Jordahl* *Pelican Rapids, Minnesota*

ASK GEORGE

I clean out and repair my nesting boxes each fall, so they're ready for birds to use as winter shelters. However, some people say I should postpone birdhouse maintenance until spring. When is the best time? —Elliot Barnes *Groton, Connecticut*

George: If you plan to leave the houses up all winter, then it's best to wait until spring to clean them. Then you can remove insects and old nesting materials from both birds and mice.

Mice tend to use birdhouses in winter and supplement the birds' nesting materials with their own. Birds also welcome the old nesting materials, as they may roost in the houses on cold winter nights.

Chapter 9
Weathering Winter

*N*o doubt about it, when Ole Man Winter arrives, feathered friends that stay for the season could use a helping hand.

So keep your feeders filled and try a few of these reader ideas to help birds weather the harshest of seasons. They'll repay you with frequent visits, add brilliance to colorless landscapes and bring lots of activity for you to view from your favorite picture window.

You'll also enjoy peace of mind knowing that your backyard birds have all that's needed for them to survive—even as you cozy up to the hot fire with a cup of steaming cocoa.

During the winter it's too difficult for us to fill our bird feeders. So we convert our window boxes into feeders.

We line them with pine boughs and place pinecones, birdseed and slices of apples and oranges on top to help supplement the birds' diets.

The quick conversion also gives me a way to get a close view of my feathered friends! —*Linda Martin Boise, Idaho*

I made my own heated birdbath by lining a 5-gallon bucket with old carpet and filling it halfway with gravel. Then, I inserted a light socket with a 60-watt lightbulb into the bucket and set a dish of water on top. (Use extreme care that you don't splash water onto the socket. Always use a GFI outlet.) The light heats the rock, which keeps the water in the dish from freezing.

—*Larry Vink, Topeka, Kansas*

I save grease from bacon and other meats in a refrigerated container. When winter gets especially frigid, I'll place the hardened fat at my feeders for my feathered friends.

—*Jill Hersch, Ayr, North Dakota*

Dark-eyed juncos don't visit unless I throw some seed on the ground. So I scatter cracked corn below my feeders. This also attracts other ground feeders like mourning doves, northern cardinals and various sparrows. —*William Yoder Guthrie, Kentucky*

Evening grosbeaks and other northern finches are specially equipped to store large amounts of seed in an internal sack called a crop. So don't be alarmed if you see them bingeing on your seed before nightfall. They're just filling their crops so they can live off the seed throughout the cold night.

—*Keith Runyon, Havana, Illinois*

In fall, I gather my homegrown pumpkins and freeze them whole. On a cold winter day, I place them outside and wait for the squirrels to come. They'll dig in, occasionally scattering some seeds to share with the birds. —*Diane Tschantz Columbus, Ohio*

I don't have a heated birdbath, but I still provide water for my feathered friends during the cold season. In the morning when the water in my birdbath is frozen, I simply pour hot water over the ice. This quickly loosens it, and I pop the ice right out of the birdbath. Then I refill it with warm water. When it's really cold, I'll do this a few times a day. —*Sherry Schoberg Elkridge, Maryland*

For a sweet winter bird treat, I tightly pack a snowball and drizzle maple syrup or honey on it. I leave a few of them on my tray feeders.
—*Anne Fauvell Rapid City, South Dakota*

Bundling up in winter to fill my feeders isn't one of my favorite chores. So I hang the feeders on shepherd's hooks within a foot of my windows. I can reach out and fill the feeders, all without leaving the warmth of my house.
—*Jodie Stevenson Export, Pennsylvania*

After a long winter, I fill my birdbath with vinegar, cover it and let it sit overnight. In the morning, I rinse it thoroughly with a hose. This helps fight the scum that built up during the cold season. —*Barbara Haynes Harwich, Massachusetts*

My vegetable garden provides an abundant food supply to birds in winter. So I leave lots of my plants in the ground. Okra is particularly popular with northern cardinals. I often see them pecking at the woody pods. White-breasted nuthatches search the stalks for insects, and downy woodpeckers rattle the plants in search of larvae. —*Jim Low Jefferson City, Missouri*

A long-handled windshield scraper makes a handy tool for cleaning bird feeders in winter. It works especially well if you have lots of tray feeders. —*Lynne McLernon Lake Geneva, Wisconsin*

In our area, many people participate in the Scandinavian Christmas tradition of hanging bundles of oats or wheat from trees for the birds.

Each year we gather and decorate bundles of wheat to give to our friends for Christmas presents. It's a great way to feed the birds, draw them close to your home and carry on this tradition. —*Darwin Anthony Trimont, Minnesota*

Becky Myers

I'm a kindergarten teacher and invited my class to my house to learn about birds. We spent a couple hours decorating my backyard to attract our feathered friends. For example, we strung edible garland and hanging ornaments made of bread slices and bagels (above). We also spread peanut butter on wooden circles I cut from plywood and rolled them in birdseed.

When finished, we gathered indoors for hot cocoa and to watch hungry birds and squirrels enjoy the treats. —*Mary Jane Coney Salem, New Hampshire*

Striped and black-oil sunflower seeds are a high-energy food that's perfect for feeding birds in winter.
—*Gloria Meredith Harrington, Delaware*

Nothing lifts my spirits like the sound of birds. But when it's cold out, I can't hear their beautiful calls. So I set up a baby monitor outside under the protection of a tray feeder.

Every evening around dusk, a northern cardinal sings us a goodnight song. It's as if the birds are in the room with us! —*Ella Vee Mayes Bedias, Texas*

Make sure winter feeders are filled at dawn and dusk. That's when the birds are stocking up on food.

During the night, they spend most of their energy, so many need to refuel first thing in the morning. They'll also load up heavily in the evening so that they have enough fuel to carry them through the cold night. —*Keith Runyon Havana, Illinois*

I made a fleece perch cover to fit over my shepherd's hook. The length doesn't matter, but leave the fuzzy side facing outward. It creates a soft warm spot for the birds to land in winter, and in spring they gather

*By George…*Nuthatches are known for stashing sunflower seeds and beef suet in the crevices of tree bark, although brown creepers, chickadees, titmice and other nuthatches are just as likely to recover the cache.

—*George Harrison, Contributing Editor*
Source: The Birds of Winter

the fluffy material to line their nests.
—*Loretta Grunewald*
Shenandoah, Virginia

To provide water for birds in winter, I fill a metal bucket with hot ash from my fireplace. Then I'll take the ash outside and set a metal dish on top of the bucket and fill it with water. The ashes keep the water from freezing for quite a while.
—*Erma Evans, Garfield, Arkansas*

Don't prune vegetation until spring. This provides more shelter and food for birds.
—*Annette MacDonald*
Hampton, Ontario

After noticing so many Christmas trees discarded near the curb, I realized they'd make terrific winter bird cover. So I dragged several into my yard, stuck them into snowbanks near my feeders and decorated them with suet treats and pinecones coated with peanut butter.
—*Darlene Doorn*
Rice Lake, Wisconsin

In the winter, fill an aluminum pie pan with a standard suet recipe and let it harden in the refrigerator. Then poke a small hole through the middle of the suet and pie pan. Insert a pipe cleaner, knot the bottom and bend the top so you can hang it from a tree branch. —*Kathryn Neuner*
Mascoutah, Illinois

During winter, I crumble the toast crusts that my four teenagers discard and toss them onto our shed roof, where my dog and the squirrels can't reach them, but birds can.
—*Therese Boileau, Hull, Quebec*

After the growing season ends, I empty my window boxes into a compost bin and turn them on their sides to use as feeding shelters. They protect the seed from wind and snow. The birds also appear comfortable dining in their protection.
—*Margaret Capstick*
Sarnia, Ontario

Dense trees and shrubs, like cedar, spruce and Japanese holly, provide birds with great protection from winter's nasty elements—snow, ice and sleet. When placed near a feeder, they also provide protection from predators.
—*Marcia Sinclair*
Marion, North Carolina

Larry Dech

We left two dead spruce trees in our yard because they provide a buffet of bugs for downy, hairy and pileated woodpeckers. —*Gina Phillips*
Wolfville, Nova Scotia

We hang a clay saucer (above) from the eaves of our house and fill it with inexpensive wild birdseed, cubed rye bread and corn bread crumbs. The overhang keeps the seed and bread dry, and we can watch the birds eat right from our window. —*Karen Dowty*
Ventura, California

Birds have to look harder to find food during winter, but not in my yard. I keep my feeder filled and provide extra plates of fruit for them. I simply set a heavy log on the ground beneath my feeder. To the log, I nail a couple aluminum pie plates and load them up with apples, oranges, raisins and cranberries.
—*Mary Farlow*
Milton, Wisconsin

Don't forget to shovel a walkway to your feeders when clearing snow from your sidewalk or driveway. This makes it a lot easier to fill empty feeders, especially when the snow begins to stack up.
—*Adrianne Wieczorek*
Orland Park, Illinois

At harvesttime, collect seeds from melons and pumpkins. Lay them out to dry and serve them to the birds during winter's coldest months. —*Gloria Meredith*
Harrington, Delaware

I set a dish filled with water on a barrel located just below a window. Because the water freezes quickly, I just open the window, remove the ice that accumulates in the dish and refill it. It's very convenient, and the birds appreciate my extra effort.
—*Margaret Retz*
Boyceville, Wisconsin

My yard is too small for a lot of trees and shrubs, so I provide another source of protection for my backyard birds. I attached latticework below my deck. The holes are large enough for small birds to slip through, but too small for predators to get in. They seem to appreciate the spacious protection below my deck. —*Bonnie Fuller*
Lead, South Dakota

Carl Sams II

A snowman can make an excellent winter bird feeder. Just replace the traditional stick arms with coneflower stalks and sprinkle birdseed on the snowman's hat and at its feet. I made the face with carrots and nuts. Birds love 'em. —*Lori Qualls*
Midland, Michigan

I make it a point to put out water for the birds several times a day in winter. I usually place a dish out in the early morning and late afternoon, during their most active feeding times. Eastern bluebirds and American robins especially like the water when they return in early spring. —*Tina Jacobs*
Wantage, New Jersey

To provide water for the birds, I fill a shallow metal pan with water and clamp an auto repair light below it. A 60-watt lightbulb keeps it thawed. —*Diana Austin*
Douglasville, Georgia

During winter, I use my picnic table as a three-tiered feeding station. I toss seed on the ground beneath the table so the birds have a sheltered place to feed. The benches and tabletop serve as tray feeders.
—*Judith Froehlich*
Berkeley Heights, New Jersey

I've fed birds suet blocks for many years. But a less expensive way to satisfy their suet appetite is to simply spread lard on the bark of trees. They love it, and it's a fun way to watch them. —*Bruce Schaffner*
Cochrane, Wisconsin

ASK GEORGE
I recently decided to replace the lard in my suet mixture with less-expensive shortening. The birds still devour it, but can you tell me if the shortening is safe for birds? —*Betty Reese*
Campton, Kentucky

George: Beef suet and lard are animal fats, while shortening is vegetable fat. Because they're all fats, birds will consume them as needed in their diets.

Although I haven't seen any scientific studies about how these fats might affect birds, I would assume shortening is just as safe—or perhaps even safer—for our feathered friends than lard, because it contains less cholesterol.

A great winter bird feeder can be built with a plastic colander. Simply string a few lengths of wire through its top holes or handles and hang it from a branch or shepherd's hook. Fill with seed and let the birds enjoy. The tiny holes allow melted snow to drain and helps the seeds dry quickly. —*Kathy Scarbro Mt. Hope, West Virginia*

In the spirit of Christmas, I decided to provide my backyard birds with a holiday stocking, too. So I filled a small one with a sprig of millet (pictured below) that I bought at the pet store. I hung the stocking on my birdhouse and prepared to take a photograph of a bird enjoying the treat. By the time I returned an hour later, the millet was entirely consumed! I guess they really appreciated my holiday gesture.

—*Jeanette McDonald Freedom, Pennsylvania*

IT'S A FACT...
Crows will fly up to 50 miles on winter nights to roost in evergreens with as many as 100,000 other crows.

For winter feeding, here's the easiest way to make suet for the birds: Collect excess cooking grease in a tin can and put it in the freezer. You can even add eggshells, cornmeal and seeds to the can as it's being filled.

When it's full, use a can opener to remove the bottom. Then punch two holes in the side of the can, near the top and bottom rims. Insert a piece of wire through the holes, wrap them around the rims and hang the can horizontally from a tree or bird feeder. (Make sure the wire won't accidentally poke your feathered friends.)

It won't take long for the birds to clean it out. —*Janet Maki Cohasset, Minnesota*

Leave a few birdhouses up during winter. Birds that don't migrate may roost in these nest boxes, especially on cold nights.

—*Gloria Meredith Harrington, Delaware*

I soak raisins in warm water so they're soft and plump. Then I set them in a dish for American robins and other ground feeders as a special winter or early spring treat.

—*Jim Hall Wichita, Kansas*

I made a wooden box and enclosed a floodlight. Then I cut an 8-inch centered circle in the box top, just large enough to fit an 8-inch clay dish. I fill the dish with water every morning, and the light keeps the water from freezing all day long.
—*Clifford Smith*
Marysville, Michigan

To protect our feeders from the elements, we strapped an umbrella to the pole of our shepherd's hook. The feeders below stay dry.
—*Shirley Savidge*
Indianapolis, Indiana

I used an old skylight to create a protected feeding station. It's supported at each corner by sturdy 4x4s. Several feeders and suet cages hang beneath the skylight.
—*Audrey Churchill*
Springfield, Oregon

Each autumn, I turn my hanging flower baskets into "birdie hotels" for roosting on cold nights. I empty the baskets, line them with soft cotton and cover it with straw. I add protective cover with oak leaves that I attach to the basket's wires. The birds can enter and exit whenever they want, and sometimes choose to use the same baskets to raise their young in spring.
—*Karen Cofer*
Gainesville, Georgia

Submersible birdbath heaters

are a quick and easy way to provide water to birds when the weather is below freezing. The best part is you can use your existing birdbath. I always place a couple large stones in the birdbath, giving them a place to land.
—*Helen Barnard*
Kalispell, Montana

After the holidays, we haul our Christmas tree outside and decorate it with goodies, like dried fruit and pinecones coated with peanut butter. We remove the top half of the tree and fasten a bird feeder to the trunk. This provides shelter *and* a feeding station for the birds, like horned larks (above).
—*Lora Rasor*
Bradford, Ohio

IT'S A FACT...

Some birds will tuck a foot inside their feathers to keep warm during winter. Often, they'll alternate feet as the exposed foot cools.

Provide extra protection at your feeders during winter by attaching wide Plexiglas roofs to your bird feeders (pictured above). They're easy to add to your existing roof, and you can still watch feathered friends dine. It's a great way to protect the birds from hawks, too.

—*Richard Snyder*
Emmaus, Pennsylvania

Years ago my husband attached a shelf just outside our window for the birds and me. I fill it with sunflower seeds and cracked corn. To fill it, all I have to do is open the window.

Our grandkids and "indoor" cats also like this close-up view of the birds. —*Maxine Witte*
Rhineland, Missouri

I offer safe shelter for birds wintering in my backyard by leaving roosting boxes and nesting ledges up year-round. They'll especially take advantage of these shelters during harsh weather.

—*Gloria Meredith*
Harrington, Delaware

In winter, we attach branches cut from cedar trees to our feeders. It provides the birds with protective cover. The simple addition seems to draw more birds to our backyard.

—*Sue Bogart, Topeka, Kansas*

We make grapevine wreaths decorated with suet balls, donuts, popcorn, cranberry garland and dried fruits. They're a hit with the birds and squirrels. We even gave one to my parents for Christmas. They loved all the activity it drew to their backyard.

—*Jay and Paula Johnson*
Duluth, Minnesota

To provide birds with water in winter, I use a heated pet dish (pictured below). It comes equipped with a thermostat and insulation. Since the bowl is quite deep, I place a rock in the water to provide a surface for the birds to stand on. The water hasn't froze yet, even when the temperature has reached -10°.

—*Roland Jordahl*
Pelican Rapids, Minnesota

I like to buy living Christmas trees so I can plant them after the holidays to add to my birdscaped backyard. But the ground is too hard to dig a hole for the root ball in late December. So I find a good spot in autumn, dig the hole and keep the collected soil in a large bucket in my garage so it stays thawed until I'm ready to plant it.

—*Tim Foster*
Barboursville, Virginia

Use Christmas cookie cutters to make birdseed ornaments. Just cut shapes from leftover bread and brush them with egg whites. Then press them in birdseed and bake at 350° for 10 minutes. Thread yarn about 1/4 inch from the tops of the ornaments and hang on trees.

—*Megan Williams*
Belleville, New York

In autumn, I gather cornstalks from my garden and weave them through loose wire fencing (at right) that I stake into a half circle around my feeders. This protects them from the prevailing wind. The stalks make a perfect winter windbreak so the birds can get out of the harsh winds while eating. They often find extra snacks in the stalks—I leave several dried ears of corn for them.

—*Glenn Orchard*
Amherstburg, Ontario

When kids get bored on winter break, pull out heavy string (like butcher string) and some treats left over from the holidays and make bird garland.

The birds particularly enjoy popcorn garland. We'll also add peanuts

RP Photo

(still in the shell), cranberries and other dried fruits.

To add the peanuts, a strong needle and thimble really helps. This treat will attract blue jays, woodpeckers and many other birds.

—*Pamela Stebbins*
Charleston, West Virginia

I've heard a lot of jokes over the years about holiday fruitcake, but around my place, the birds are the ones that get the last laugh.

We place fruitcake leftovers in our suet feeders and never lack for visitors—woodpeckers, mockingbirds and blue jays seem to love this treat.

I've even made my own for them with finely chopped nuts and dried fruit. But most of the time there's plenty left at the end of the holidays!
—*Marion Little, Humboldt, Indiana*

Birds love fruit in winter. I'll offer apples, grapes, cherries, oranges, bananas and grapefruits—whatever's on sale at the grocery store.

Cut round fruits, like apples and oranges, into 1/2-inch disks. This makes it easier for them to eat because they won't rock or slide around on the feeding tray.
—*Ron Adler, St. Peters, Missouri*

Use sunflower heads and evergreen trimmings to make all-natural wreaths for the birds. I use the dried sunflower in the center and arrange the branches around it. Then I decorate it with edible garland and other treats. —*Justine Morris*
Ravenna, Ohio

IT'S A FACT...
Peanut butter is a good cold-weather treat for birds because they need extra fat in their diet to keep warm. And, contrary to popular belief, it's perfectly safe for the birds—they *won't* choke on it.

Chapter 10
Watch the Birdie

*G*reat bird photographs don't just happen. They take planning, patience and skill. Most importantly, you have to find a way to get up close and personal with your feathered friends—even if they're skittish by nature.

Several readers have found ways to compose award-winning photographs by working *with* backyard birds. And, for the most part, these tricks don't require new or fancy camera equipment, just some clever thinking and lots of film.

Photo: Lance Beeny

The best time to photograph birds is early morning and late afternoon. That's when the birds most often eat. Plus, that's when daylight will give you the richest color.
—*Diana Kidd, Alexandria, Virginia*

A handheld shutter release on my SLR (single-lens-reflex) camera means I can sit a few feet from my camera that's mounted on a tripod (see photo below). This seems to

make the birds more comfortable. I focus the camera on a place where the birds frequently perch.
—*Frank Boster Jr., Delaware, Ohio*

I anchored a heavy cedar post near my picture window just for the birds. On the side, I drilled a hole to hold suet mix. The hole is positioned so that it's nearly invisible as I take great profiles of the birds. The pictures of the downy and red-bellied

woodpeckers (below left) are two of my favorites.   —*Eugene Westley Lemon Springs, North Carolina*

Always keep a camera close by and loaded with film. I even keep my camera with me in the car. You never know when you'll see an interesting bird worth photographing.
—*Georgia Stewart, Hebron, Illinois*

Pay attention to the sun. If it's in your frame, it'll create a glare and ruin the shot. A lens "hood" sometimes helps.   —*Belinda Norris Slater, Missouri*

It's easier to get great shots of beautiful tropical wading birds (like this roseate spoonbill below) in our

backyard when we work together. One of us carries the camera and the other totes extra equipment.
—*Vivian and Dick Stanton Clearwater, Florida*

Attach a stick near your bird feeder. Most birds will perch on it before and after they eat, which gives you more chances for that elusive photograph.   —*Wendell Obermeier Charles City, Iowa*

Bonnie Nance

Take It from a Pro

ONE of our frequently published photographers, Bonnie Nance of Owensboro, Kentucky, was happy to share some of her basic tips for ensuring great avian photographs. Here's a handful that should help you produce flawless photos:

• Single-lens-reflex (SLR) cameras allow you to experiment with interchangeable lenses—especially telephoto lenses for close-up photographs of birds.

• A tripod is a must when using telephoto lenses because camera movement blurs photographs.

• There are more than 100 different 35mm films on the market. When choosing one, be sure to consider the ISO number printed on the film box.

The lower the ISO number (25, 50, 100), the more light is required to expose the film, but they also give the richest color and highest quality. A higher number (200, 400, 1600) indicates a more sensitive or "faster" film. Faster films may produce photographs that are blur-free, but have more contrast and grain than the slower films.

• Just before sunset is a great time to take pictures. You can position the camera so the low sun is behind your photo subject (called "backlighting") or coming in from either side ("sidelighting"). The results can be quite dramatic.

• Avoid midday photography, when bright direct sunlight washes out the birds' colors.

For fabulous close-up bird photos, use a garage, barn or shed as a photo blind.

I set up several bird feeders and birdbaths near my outbuilding and cut several holes in the wall facing the feeding area.

Make sure the holes are large enough for your camera's lens and cut each one at a different height. Then place a stool inside near the holes so you can be comfortable while waiting for your feathered friends to take their positions. —*Kathy Lockwood St. Johns, Michigan*

I've had great success photographing birds from my own homemade photo blinds. Here are some "secrets" to help you take better bird portraits:

• Build a movable blind from a wooden pallet. Attach plywood sides to it and paint several trees on it so that it blends in with the surroundings. Cut holes in the plywood for your telephoto lens.

• Cardboard appliance boxes make perfect photo blinds. Just don't leave them outside when you're finished. They won't stand up to the weather.

• As you prepare to shoot photographs from a photography blind, always have someone walk to it with you, and then leave once you're set. Birds can't count, so when they see someone walk away, they'll think the "coast is clear". You'll be surprised at the increased bird activity. —*Emanuel Schlabach Winesburg, Ohio*

For great hummingbird photos, always cover all but one feeding port at your sugar-water feeder. I'll use clear marbles or scotch tape to cov-

er the ports. That way, I know exactly where they'll feed and where to focus. —*Len Eisenzimmer Portland, Oregon*

I love to photograph nestlings, especially at feeding time. Before I take pictures, however, I make sure the bird family (such as these gray catbirds below) doesn't mind my intrusion.

I'll first stand in the area where I plan to set up my camera and wait to

see if the adult birds become agitated. If they don't mind, I'll return with my equipment.
—*Hubert Brandenburg Hagerstown, Maryland*

I use a doubler, also called a "2X teleconverter", to get close-up bird photos. This allows me to convert my 70-210mm zoom lens into a 140-

Photography blinds can be made out of anything. I made mine from my daughter's play tent and draped it with a secondhand camouflage tarp. (I placed a shower curtain below it so I would stay dry in winter.)

Christina Kidd

Be sure the tarp is tightly fastened to the frame to prevent it from blowing in the wind, which may scare wildlife.

Here are a few more tips I've learned from my experience with photo blinds:

• Leave the blind in the same spot for a few days. This gives the birds a chance to get used to it. Initially, they may avoid your yard until they become acclimated to your blind.

• When photographing from a blind, you'll probably be outside for a long period of time. You may want to bring some of these items with you: Tissues, padded cushions, a blanket, a radio with headphones, extra film, more batteries and an insulated container with something to drink. —*Diana Kidd, Alexandria, Virginia*

420mm zoom lens. Because I stand farther away from them, the birds are more comfortable.
—*Frank Boster Jr., Delaware, Ohio*

To make personal greeting cards, take your best bird photographs to

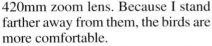

Have a hummerdinger BIRTHDAY!

a photo center and customize them. You can add your own personal messages above, below or over the photograph and print it in different sizes. You can also add handwritten

text to your photographs with a permanent marker (see photo below left). —*Pam White
Huntsville, Alabama*

The best way to get clear and close bird photos is to use a photo blind. They can be as simple as a family tent, or a covered wooden frame that fits two chairs and a tripod.
—*Jay Fulkerson
Woodville, New York*

IT'S A FACT...

If you enjoy photographing birds from a window, leave your camera set up where you plan to shoot your photos. The birds will get used to it, and you'll have a chance to get better pictures.

Rick and Nora Bowers

Before photographing hummingbirds, pay careful attention to their favorite places to perch and feed. Because they move so quickly, it's good to have an idea where they might land next. Once you're familiar with their flight and perching patterns, you'll find it's much easier to photograph them.
—*Wendell Obermeier*
Charles City, Iowa

For a quick photo blind, use a freestanding clothing rack, 30-gallon black plastic garbage bag and some tape. Cut one side and the bottom of the garbage bag so you can open it like a plastic sheet, and tape it to the top and sides of the rack.

Position your camera on a tripod and cut an "X" in the plastic at the height of your lens, and push it through the hole. I photograph a lot of hummingbirds this way.
—*Pam White, Huntsville, Alabama*

I've made several simple and inexpensive photo blinds from tarps over the years. Just build a set of stands from old lumber or use two wooden 6-foot stepladders as supports. Then attach a tarp between them. Cut several "L-shaped" openings in the tarp at different heights

for your camera lens. These openings work best because the L-shaped flaps "flop" downward, automatically closing when not in use. This hides me better when I'm behind the blind.
—*Jenny Butenhoff*
Franklin, Wisconsin

I take my favorite bird photos and put them in basic picture frames. Then I glue decorative flowers (like the ones found at most crafting stores) or other natural items that I find in the backyard (acorns, pinecones, etc.) around the frames. I like to use colors that complement the

Great bird photos can be taken through a picture window. Here are a few basic rules to help get sparkling results:
- Shoot with your lens as close to the glass as possible.
- Turn off indoor lights.
- Remove all screens.
- Wash your window so it is crystal clear both inside and out.
- Wear dark clothing.
- Collect interesting branches and rocks and set an outside scene to your liking. This is your chance to "design nature".
- Place suet and bird feeders near natural cover. As the birds approach the feeders, they'll land in this cover, and you can photograph them in their natural settings.
- Keep your photo equipment nearby. You'll be able to catch those special moments that are least expected.
—*Diana Kidd*
Alexandria, Virginia

bird in the photo. It's a really nice way to show off your photographs!
—*Kendra Jackson, Bronx, New York*

If a wild bird flies away when it sees you approach with a camera, don't give up. Stand still and wait— it'll probably return and accept you in its territory when it feels safe.
—*Belinda Norris, Slater, Missouri*

Don't be stingy with film. Keep clicking, and you'll have a larger selection of shots to choose from.
—*Laurie Lewis*
Waltham, Massachusetts

I set my feeders near brush piles and trees. This gives me an opportunity to photograph birds (like this cedar waxwing below) in their natural settings as they rest among the branches.
—*Stanley Buman*
Carroll, Iowa

Birds like these morning doves (below) will stay in your yard longer if you provide a couple sources of

water. This will give you more chances to take award-winning photographs.
—*Mary Farlow*
Milton, Wisconsin

Sit near your feeder for a while each time you refill it. Soon the birds will accept you as part of the landscape. You'll find photographing them will be much easier.
—*Stefan Delloff*
Pequannock, New Jersey

Birds don't pose, so keep shooting. You'll end up throwing away a lot of extra pictures, but it's worth it for a few excellent ones!
—*Mary Welty*
Denver, North Carolina

To photograph woodpeckers, build a sturdy tray-style feeder (like mine above left) with a large log mounted vertically to its top. Build a wide base so it won't tip, but make it portable so you can move it wherever you want.

The log gives the photos (like these red-bellied woodpeckers) a natural look. *—Russ McPhee Brigden, Ontario*

I placed my feeding station about 18 feet from my home office window. That's just about the perfect distance for taking photos with my long telephoto lenses (300 to 500mm) through the glass.

—Roland Jordahl Pelican Rapids, Minnesota

Avoid distractions in the background of your photos, especially when using a telephoto lens. These long lenses bring the background closer to your subject, so it's important to keep this in mind when composing your shots.

—Diana Kidd, Alexandria, Virginia

If you can change your camera's lenses, the best way to get close to wildlife is to use a doubler or tripler (also called a 2X or 3X teleconverter), which is an inexpensive device that mounts between your camera and the lens. It allows you to zoom in much closer.

—Richard Howard Tucson, Arizona

Use a tripod when taking bird photos. Any camera movement will alter the clarity of your photographs. Zoom and telephoto lenses increase the chances of camera movement. *—Tony Sowers Milo, Iowa*

When photographing birds, position yourself and your camera at the level of the subject. If you see an American robin pulling up a plump worm (below), lay on your stomach and take the picture from ground level. *—Brandy LaFountain Marion, Michigan*

Mark P. Saunders

Here's a trick to get great bird photos. I set up a tripod several feet away from my feeders with a small black wooden box mounted to it. I inch it closer over the span of a couple days so the birds become accustomed to the device. Once activity is back to normal, I replace the black box with my camera. A re-

ASK GEORGE

I like using flash photography when taking pictures of birds because the colors and details become more vibrant. Is there a way to shoot flash photographs of birds from inside my picture window? This would be especially helpful in winter.
—Margaret Krueger
New Berlin, Wisconsin

George: When using a flash while shooting through a window, hold the flash flat against the glass to prevent the reflection from bouncing back. The only extra equipment you'll need is a cord that allows you to remove the flash from your camera.

Before buying extra equipment, you may want to try moving your camera lens as close to the window as possible while leaving the flash mounted to the camera. This also may eliminate the reflections.

---

mote cord (an accessory on some cameras) allows me to snap pictures from within a blind or from inside my house. —*Jo Ann Sheldon*
Arkansas City, Kansas

To give the illusion that birds are in a forest and not your backyard, adorn a feeding tray with various sizes of tree branches.
—*Jay Fulkerson*
Woodville, New York

Use a fast shutter speed when taking pictures of birds. They're constantly moving, and a slow shutter speed will create blurry photographs. I choose a shutter speed of 1/250th of a second or faster.
—*Mary Welty*
Denver, North Carolina

To photograph American goldfinches in my backyard, I removed my bathroom window screen and

put my camera on the windowsill. My bathroom makes a perfect blind.
—*Kris Bisson*
Honey Brook, Pennsylvania

The secret to taking amazing bird photos is to get close. I found the best way to do this is to use a "bag blind" that drapes over your body. You can buy them or make them out of camouflage fabric. Be sure to cut a hole at the top for your camera lens to fit through. It's the most economical and portable blind I've found. —*Paul McAfee*
Fort Wayne, Indiana

IT'S A FACT...

Bird photographs make fantastic Christmas cards. Many photo processors will produce holiday cards from your negatives or slides.

Al Cornell

Take several photos of each bird you photograph. They may unexpectedly turn their head, ruffle their feathers or open their bill mid-shot. Odds are, you'll get a good picture (like the one of this hungry blue jay below) if you're not stingy with film.

—Hubert Brandenburg
Hagerstown, Maryland

I use a flash when taking pictures of birds—even on sunny days. The flash seems to make the birds really "stand out" in my photos.

—Marsha Melder
Shreveport, Louisiana

Freeze motion by using a flash. Be sure you have the perfect composition and settings because the birds might not immediately return for a second shot.

Another way to get crisp pictures is by using a fast shutter speed—1/250th of a second or faster.

—Diana Kidd, Alexandria, Virginia

IT'S A FACT...
Cold winter weather can cause battery-operated cameras to malfunction. Keep the batteries in a warm pocket and load them into you camera when you're ready to shoot.

Pay careful attention to the background of your photograph. Keep it uncluttered—you may only need to move the camera a few inches to get rid of the distraction. But the extra effort is worth it.

—Mary Welty
Denver, North Carolina

By George... Telephoto lenses are not always necessary for good bird photographs. With a little patience, you should be able to train your birds to feed close to your windows...and your point-and-shoot camera inside the glass.
—George Harrison, Contributing Editor

Chapter 11
Flight Safety

*N*o one likes to see feathered friends injured because of window collisions and other avoidable mishaps. So it's not surprising readers have devised all sorts of unique ways to create bird-safe flyways near their home.

This collection of reader tips contains plenty of simple solutions to take the *pane* out of backyard bird havens. You're sure to find one that's perfect for your place.

To keep birds from colliding with our picture window, I use this simple method. Fasten a nail on each side of the window frame—pounding it in just enough so it's secure. Then I rest a thin piece of wood across the nails and tie narrow strips of cloth to it.

The cloth moves in the breeze, breaking up the reflection that often tricks birds into thinking the glass isn't there.　—*Betsy Rogers*
Puyallup, Washington

Compact discs dangling from the eaves above my window signal birds to steer clear.　—*Janice Feehan*
Manteno, Illinois

I make my own bird-shaped window "clings" to help feathered friends better see my windows. I cut out the shapes from colorful plastic wrap, then paint them with fabric paint to look like birds. Once they dry, I stick them on the glass…works like a charm.　—*Mrs. Calep Davis*
Wathena, Kansas

I attached a plastic spider web on my window (they're available from Droll Yankees). The birds still visit my yard, but don't hit that window anymore.　—*P. Hubbard*
Corydon, Indiana

When a bird flies into my window, I leave the bird on the ground and place a large plastic laundry basket over it, weighing it down with a brick or rock. This protects the bird from predators while it recovers from the collision.

When it seems alert and ready to fly, I remove the basket so it can take off to safety.　—*Betsy Kinney*
Asheboro, North Carolina

I planted a small tree in front of my picture window after birds kept crashing into it. Not only did the solution stop the collisions, but I'm now able to take close-up photos through the glass as birds perch on the tree's limbs.　—*Becky Mohr*
Marathon, New York

To prevent birds from flying into our windows, we fasten silhouettes of hawks or owls on the glass (above). So far, it's worked.
　—*Charis Dankert*
La Selva Beach, California

After I stood outside my window and looked at it from a bird's-eye point of view, I could understand why birds sometimes collided with the glass—I could see straight through to the other side of my yard! To birds, it must have looked like they could fly right in.

To avert further confusion, I rearranged some of the furniture, closed an inner door and pulled the shades on one side of the house.
　—*Robert Muller*
Stony Brook, New York

I hang decorative glass sun catchers in the windows. This keeps birds from crashing into them.
—*Ruth Lindbloom*
Newberg, Oregon

The fruit-bearing vines and shrubs I planted below my window keep the birds from flying into it. They're drawn to the berries instead of the reflection. —*Clara Belle Tye*
Washougal, Washington

This idea has saved many feathered friends from close encounters with my windows.

First I attach small screw eyes about 1 foot apart around the entire window frame, making sure the eyes are directly across from each other from left to right and top to bottom. Then I thread string through the eyes and stretch it straight across the window to form a grid. As the final touch, I place colored craft beads on the strings wherever they intersect.

The criss-crossing lines and bright beads serve as a warning to birds.
—*Samuel Skaggs*
Heath, Ohio

I placed Velcro around the frame of our picture window and used it to attach fine netting across the window. The netting is nearly invisible, but it's just enough to break up reflections. When it's time to clean the windows, the netting easily lifts off.
—*Connie Ball*
Heidelberg, Mississippi

Bright-yellow "smiley face" decals bring a little happiness to my backyard and prevent birds from hitting my windows. The birds seem to spot the decals immediately and avoid running into the glass.
—*Arlene Brisbin, Perry, Ohio*

We installed 1- x 4-inch boards along the trim on each side of our windows. Then we stretched a piece of black nylon screen from one board to the other and stapled it to the boards. We attached the boards with screws, so we can easily remove them to wash the window (see illustration at right).

The screen is barely noticeable from inside. And since we installed these "bird barriers", we haven't had a single injured bird.

Even if a bird did strike it, we think the 3-inch gap between the screen and the window would create a safe cushion.
—*Rosemarie Weber*
Cleveland, North Carolina

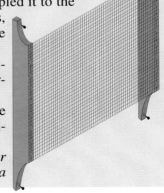

Birds don't fly into my patio door since I placed a bike flag in front of it (above). The triangular flag sways freely on its flexible pole, which is anchored several inches into the ground. It works great, and the flag was inexpensive, too.
—*Sherrie Post, Clayton, California*

I keep my backyard bird friendly by providing cover from predators.

I build brush piles close to the feeders, making sure they're far enough away so cats can't use them as springboards. I also wrap wire fencing with 2-inch openings around shrubs where small songbirds like to gather. This keeps larger birds from getting through.
—*Maggie Wright*
Chatham, New York

To protect songbirds from the hawks that sometimes frequent my backyard, I hang my bird feeders under a beautiful garden arbor.
—*Dodie Amenta*
Santa Ynez, California

ASK GEORGE

For the last 5 years, a male cardinal has been repeatedly flying into my friend's bedroom window from dawn until about noon. It happens every season except summer, when she has a screen on the window. What can she do to stop this bird?
—*Patricia Bonneau*
Lewiston, Maine

George: Male and female northern cardinals often fight their own reflections in windows because they're trying to chase the "other bird" from their nesting territory. American robins, northern mockingbirds and other birds will do the same thing.

To alleviate this problem, eliminate the reflection by soaping the window or hanging streamers of some kind outside it. Or, simply leave the screen on all year long. If that doesn't work, try covering the window from the outside.

Chapter 12
Squirrel Beaters

*L*ove 'em or hate 'em, squirrels are here to stay. And as long as they're around, no bird feeder is safe.

Luckily, *Birds & Blooms* readers are more than eager to share their thrifty and clever solutions to keep these quick-footed rascals at bay. Many of these tried-and-true ideas utilize basic materials and scraps you probably have lying around your house,

garage or basement. From milk jugs to fishing line, soap to Vaseline, each idea has one goal in mind—to keep these furry critters from devouring birdseed!

Not every solution will work in your backyard, of course. But you may find a few that will keep these furry bandits grounded—at least long enough so that you can plan phase two in this never-ending backyard battle.

Photo: Caryl May

Squirrels don't stand a chance against my feeders. I attached a 2-foot-long stovepipe to the bottom of the feeders. They crawl up the pole, but can't figure out how to make their way around the stovepipe!

—*Anita Syfert*
Locust Grove, Virginia

A paste made from 1 tablespoon cooking oil and 1 teaspoon red pepper keeps squirrels at bay. We apply the mixture to our feeder and

ASK GEORGE
Do squirrels remember where they hide their nuts?

—*Brian Sienko*
Franklin, Wisconsin

George: Squirrels will uncover buried nuts when food becomes scarce in winter. They use their keen sense of smell to find them, and can even locate those buried under several inches of snow. Odds are, however, that they'll find another squirrel's buried nut.

wooden pole with a paintbrush. The squirrels won't touch them.

—*Deane Taylor*
Summerfield, North Carolina

I string an old 33-rpm record just above my hanging feeder. Make sure it flops easily so that the squirrels can't balance on it.

—*Helen Sweltz, Cleveland, Ohio*

Use a child's water gun to squirt the squirrels when they attempt to eat from your bird feeders. It only takes a few times to train the "regulars" not to go near the feeders.

—*Dave and Marge Gelvin*
Toulon, Illinois

Sprinkle used cat litter on the ground below your feeders. I guarantee the squirrels will look for other feeders far from your backyard.

—*John Baer, Blairsville, Georgia*

Locate post-mounted feeders at least 10 feet away from trees, houses or fences. Squirrels can jump far, but not that far!

—*Harriet Swanson*
State College, Pennsylvania

I've read that hanging pieces of Irish Spring bar soap deters deer from eating gardeners' prize plants. So, I decided to try it to stop squirrels, too.

I cut pieces of the soap and slipped them into old panty hose. Then I hung the soap from small hooks on the sides of my feeders. I haven't seen a squirrel on them since.
—*Ann Carpenter*
Waukesha, Wisconsin

A simple tin can with a hinged top (below) was the answer to my squirrel problems. I attached it near my feeding station and filled it with nuts. The squirrels are so fascinated with opening and closing the can, selecting a nut and eating it that they forget about our bird feeders!

> —*Rebecca King*
> *Burlison, Tennessee*

Periodically apply a coat of Vaseline to your bird feeder poles. It's hilarious to watch the squirrels slide down the slippery pole the first time they try to climb it!

> —*Jo-An Lee Jacobs*
> *Darien, Connecticut*

Wrap sheet metal around a wooden bird feeder post. My husband wrapped a 4-foot section

---

IT'S A FACT...
Squirrels have home ranges of less than 1 acre up to 20 acres. Their ranges may overlap with other squirrels.

around our post, starting just below the feeder. The squirrels spend all day looking up at it, knowing they can't sneak past the slippery surface.

> —*Diane Eubanks*
> *Smyrna, Georgia*

Hang small wind chimes from the bottom your bird feeders. The sound of the chimes frightens squirrels, but doesn't bother the birds.

> —*Carol Draper*
> *Little Rock, Arkansas*

A wire strung from my house to a tree holds all my feeders. Squirrels may be great acrobats, but they can't walk on this high wire!

> —*L.O. Kuper, Council Bluffs, Iowa*

Spicy red pepper sprinkled in your birdseed will keep squirrels away.

> —*Peggy Cason*
> *Plain Dealing, Louisiana*

By constructing a baffle for our bird feeder pole and adding a squirrel feeding station nearby, we've eliminated the problem of the furry critters stealing birdseed.

> —*Melinda and*
> *Jim Emerson*
> *DeMotte, Indiana*

Cut a hole or an "X" through the bottom of three 1-gallon plastic milk jugs and slide the jugs over the your feeder pole. The squirrels can climb over two jugs, but not three.
—*Earlene and Dorothy Moser*
Berne, Indiana

Corncob squirrel feeders help keep those furry creatures off my bird feeders. When I run out of cobs, I take two empty tuna or cat food cans and drill a centered hole in the bottoms. Slide the first can upside down onto the nail or screw that holds the cob, and place the second can on top of the first one so it's right-side up. Fill the can with peanuts, sunflower or pumpkin seeds to keep these critters happy.
—*Margaret Doyle*
Raleigh, North Carolina

I hang my bird feeders from garage door cable. The slippery cord is impossible for squirrels to climb down.   —*Nanci Stankus*
North Smithfield, Rhode Island

A squirrel baffle kept the critters off our feeder for a short time. So did a plastic bottle that we slid onto our feeder's pole. But neither completely stopped the squirrels until we combined the contraptions (at left). Together they're a perfect pair. So far, no squirrel has beat it!
—*Pat Milner*
Livingston, Texas

We hung our feeders from a string stretching from one tree to another, but that didn't keep the squirrels from reaching our birdseed. So my husband, George (above), strung a pizza pan on both ends by drilling a small hole into the center of each pan. The squirrels haven't tried to get past them yet.   —*Sue Klein, Quitman, Texas*

I build squirrel-proof feeders for pennies! Above each hanging bird feeder, I string three old record albums separated by 3-inch pieces of plastic hose. The holes in the records are larger than the string, making them very unstable. The squirrels can't balance on them.
—*Jacqueline Fretwell*
St. Augustine, Florida

IT'S A FACT...
If you think you have too many squirrels in your backyard, here's why. It's normal for the critters to have two litters—one in the winter and another in the summer. Each litter will have three to five youngsters!

My feeders hang from a horizontal wire. To keeps squirrels from walking the wire, I placed plastic closet pole covers between the feeders. The plastic tubes roll on the wire, making it impossible for the critters to cross. But it's a lot of fun watching them try!
—*Marian Buttler, Cleveland, Ohio*

The best way to keep squirrels out of your backyard is to get a dog.
—*Tony Sowers, Milo, Iowa*

The squirrels leave our feeders alone as long as we provide a snack just for them. So I attach plastic spoons from various length strings, dipping each spoon into peanut but-

ter (above). The strings are tied onto a rope that's suspended between two trees. They pull up a spoon from the rope above, and amuse themselves for hours. —*Bonnie Proke Logan Lake, British Columbia*

Squirrels don't like safflower seeds. We've even seen one taste the seed and immediately take it out of its mouth. Safflower costs more than

Nail copper flashing around the base of your feeders and feeding trays (as pictured at right). Ours is about 8 inches deep, and squirrels can't get past it.
—*Cindy Sauve Eliot, Maine*

other seeds, but saves us money in the long run because the squirrels won't eat it, but the birds will.
—*Joe and Helen Hafter Shreveport, Louisiana*

I hang my feeders from a thin rope tied between two trees to keep them out of the squirrels' reach. They're about 5 to 6 feet off the ground, making them easy to fill.
—*Angelin Ham Jamestown, North Carolina*

This old 1970s lamp frame (at right) makes the perfect squirrel-resistant feeder post. The slippery pole is only about 1-1/2 inches in diameter, but it's quite tall. I removed all the wiring and hung feeders from each of the hooks.

—*Ernest White Brandon, Manitoba*

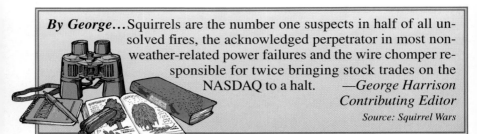

By George... Squirrels are the number one suspects in half of all unsolved fires, the acknowledged perpetrator in most non-weather-related power failures and the wire chomper responsible for twice bringing stock trades on the NASDAQ to a halt. —*George Harrison*
Contributing Editor
Source: Squirrel Wars

Hang a wind chime on the branch from which your feeders hang. When a squirrel scampers across the branch, the chimes ring and send the furry critter back in the direction from which it came.

—*Rose Kovalevich*
Newark, Delaware

We mix Irish Spring soap shavings with birdseed. This seems to prevent excessive feeder raids from the bushy-tailed squirrels. —*Ruth Royals*
Hiawassee, Georgia

Galvanized wire that's about 1/16-inch thick works great for

Place two 1-gallon milk jugs bottom-to-bottom above your hanging feeders to keep squirrels away (right).

Poke a hole in the center of each jug's bottom, then run the string or chain through it.

—*Larry and Margaret Bonnici*
Northville, Michigan

hanging feeders. The wire is too thin for the squirrels to climb down, yet plenty strong to hold the feeders.

—*John Joseph, Goshen, Ohio*

"Peppered" birdseed is seasoned with cayenne and other hot peppers. I mix this seed with thistle and sunflower seeds, and the squirrels leave it alone.

Don't rub your eyes after handling the peppered seed, or you'll understand why the squirrels refuse to touch it. —*Leslie Ball*
Millersville, Maryland

I keep pesky squirrels out of my hopper feeders by hammering nails about 1/4 inch apart along the wooden feeding trough. The nails act like jail bars, keeping the squirrels from stealing the birdseed.

—*W. Woody Breedlove*
Bangor, Maine

We hammered nails through the base of our tray feeder so the points face up. Each nail is spaced about 2 inches apart. The squirrels don't mess with this feeder. But the birds don't seem to mind the nails and can maneuver between them.

—*Bob and Joy Curry*
Niceville, Florida

Here's a dynamic duo for beating the squirrels. Place a 2-liter soda bottle around your feeder post (you may have to cut a hole in the top and bottom of the bottle) and hold it in place. Then, above the bottle, place an aluminum pie pan face down (cut a hole in the center of the pan large enough to fit around the pole). Even if the squirrels can climb past the soda bottle, they seem to stop at the flimsy and noisy pan.

—*Gerry Karg*
Riverdale, New Jersey

An 18-inch metal garbage can lid makes a great squirrel baffle for my hanging feeder (below). Wrap 10-

inch-wide aluminum flashing along the lid's lip and secure it with sheet metal screws or pop rivets. Make a hole in the center to slip over a post or the wire holding your hanging feeder.

—*Irene and George Manelski*
Pleasant Valley, New York

Place a 2-foot-long section of stovepipe halfway up your feeder's pole (right). At the bottom of the pipe, cut several 8-inch slits and bend them horizontal. This creates a barrier that squirrels can't pass.

—*Bob and Joann Hoffman*
Gladwin, Michigan

Make a squirrel baffle from an aluminum pie pan. Cut from the edge of the pan to the center. Then cut a hole in the center that's large enough to fit around your bird-feeder post.

Slide the pan around the post and use duct tape to close the slit in the pan. Wrap the pole with tape just below the pan to keep it in place. This baffle is much cheaper than the ones sold in stores.

—*Vern and Irma Flitter*
Pemberton, Minnesota

Slide a 5-quart plastic ice cream bucket upside down over your feeder's post to keep the squirrels from reaching the birdseed. It works like a charm.

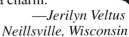

—*Jerilyn Veltus*
Neillsville, Wisconsin

Squirrels love store-bought suet cakes, but seem to avoid all-natural beef suet. Therefore, I only serve birds the real stuff. Freeze any extra beef suet to keep it from going bad.

—*Diana Kidd*
Alexandria, Virginia

Mount tray-style feeders on PVC pipe. I use 10-foot lengths of 3-inch pipe and bury it 3 feet into the ground. Attach a plastic or cast iron

bracket to the bottom of your feeder that fits over the 3-inch diameter pipe. I haven't had a problem with squirrels since I began using this method. It's been 10 years!

To fill the tall feeders, screw an old coffee can (through its bottom) to a 4-foot-long scrap board (see photo at left). I simply fill the can with seed and tip it into the tray.

—*Russell Van Nostrand*
Marshalls Creek, Pennsylvania

Mix the seeds of extremely hot peppers into your birdseed. You'll instantly keep squirrels out of the feeders. They can't stand the spicy taste, but it has no effect on birds because they can't taste it. Be sure to use gloves and don't touch your face or eyes. —*Marilyn Wittkamper*
Anderson, Indiana

Our squirrels are accomplished tightrope walkers, easily mastering the clothesline from which our bird feeders are hung. So I strung several empty spools from sewing thread

Birds can't taste hot peppers or hot sauce, and it provides additional vitamin C for them. So, this suet recipe is ideal if squirrels are raiding your suet cages:

1 pound lard
16-20 ounces peanut butter
1 cup raisins
1/8 to 1/4 cup dried red pepper flakes
1/8 cup cayenne pepper hot sauce
1 cup wild birdseed
6 cups cornmeal
5 cups flour

In a saucepan, melt the lard over medium heat. Remove it from the heat and add peanut butter, raisins, red pepper and hot sauce. Mix until the peanut butter melts. Add remaining ingredients and mix well. Pack into bread pans and chill. Remove cooled brick from pan and slice. —*Julian Foster, Indialantic, Florida*

onto the line. Those sneaky critters have now been stopped.
—*Joan Nichols*
Deep River, Ontario

The sound of music surrounds my bird feeders because I hang them from old guitar strings. The skinny and slippery strings stump the squirrels. They obviously don't have the gift of song. —*Bob Poling*
Perry, Ohio

A "Slinky" toy surrounds our bird feeder pole (left). It keeps the pesky squirrels from climbing it.
—*Betty Sharrock*
Johnston,
South Carolina

I hang my bird feeders directly below our patio roof. The squirrels can't jump or climb to them, and it brings the birds in really close.
—*Mary Em McGlone*
Philadelphia, Pennsylvania

Squirrels can't overcome the 2-liter soft drink bottles surrounding my feeder's pole. I cut a hole in the bottom of each bottle and stack them on the 3/4-inch metal feeder pole. —*Doris Petschow*
Venice, Florida

I wrapped spiraled phone wire to the pole of a bird feeder. The squirrels won't climb it because they don't like the springy addition.
—*Shirley Kimmerle-O'Donnell*
McDonald, Pennsylvania

> **IT'S A FACT...**
> *Birds & Blooms* reader Harry Pederson of Vergas, Minnesota, accidentally discovered a squirrel's winter stash buried in a pile of topsoil in his backyard. So he counted how many nuts were in that secret hiding place—3,161 to be exact!
>
> As you would expect, Harry gave the entire heap back to his resident squirrel.
>
> "Within a few days, they were all gone," he says.

When I finish a jar of peanut butter, I leave the lid on and cut the plastic jar in half. Then I place the two containers in my yard. It keeps the squirrels busy for days.
—*S. Caronna, Enfield, Connecticut*

Create a double barrier to keep squirrels from raiding your suet. Load the suet into a small suet cage,

then place it in a larger one (above). Now the squirrels can't get to the suet cakes, but the birds have no trouble reaching through with their bills. —*Bonita Laettner*
Angola, New York

Squirrels won't even attempt to try accessing my hanging bird feeder. Two 2-liter soft-drink bottles (one with the bottom removed) sits atop the feeder (left). The feeder's hanging string runs through the plastic bottles. Of course, this will only work with a roofed feeder like mine, but it works great!

—*Merl Phillips*
Eagleville, Tennessee

We sunk two 10-foot vertical 1-inch pipes about 2 feet into the ground, placing them several feet from each other. We put a domed squirrel baffle on each pipe before connecting the poles with a horizontal crossbar above the baffles.

We hang our feeders from the crossbar. The baffles prevent the squirrels from climbing the pipe to get to the feeders. Plus, they're mounted high enough to keep them out of the squirrels' reach.

—*Maryjoan and Keith Sena*
Iselin, New Jersey

We wrap chicken wire around our post-mounted feeders. Tuck the ends beneath the feeder so the birds don't get poked. Simply unfold it to refill. It's not beautiful, but it keeps the larger birds and squirrels from devouring the seed. —*Karen Pyle*
Moscow, Idaho

Hang bird feeders from 40-pound monofilament fishing line. Be sure to leave 10 feet of room on each side of the feeder. If there's a tree, fence or other structure closer than that, the squirrel may be able to jump to it. —*Maurice Lachapelle*
Monmouth, Maine

Here's an easy way to turn a bucket into a squirrel baffle. Cut an "X" in the center of the bucket's bot-

---

ASK GEORGE

I've heard that adding cayenne pepper to birdseed to repel squirrels and other wildlife can irritate membranes in birds' mouths and throats, eventually causing them to die. Is this true?
—*Dulcie Fralin*
Wilmington, North Carolina

George: Cayenne pepper has no apparent effect on birds, whose sense of taste and smell is not

well developed. Its effect on squirrels is also in question; I've tried it at my feeders and squirrels seem unaffected by the pepper.

tom. Slide it upside down onto the post and drill a hole into each triangular tab and into the post. Secure the bucket with sheet-metal screws.
—*Mary Joe Thomas*
Stonewall, Louisiana

When we keep our squirrel feeders full, the critters leave our bird feeders alone. We provide a decorative bench loaded with sunflower

seeds (above). We've realized the best way to make our backyard visitors happy is to have something for all of them. —*Emilia Williams*
West Pubnico, Nova Scotia

I made a 28-inch-long feeder hook from an ordinary wire shirt hanger. Just snip off the hook and straighten the hanger. Use pliers to bend a hook on each end, so you can hang the feeder from a branch. For some reason, the squirrels can't climb down this wire. —*Ila Price*
Jacksonville, Illinois

Vicks VapoRub is my secret to keeping squirrels from my bird feeders. I grease up the post with the smelly stuff. They end up sliding down on their first try and don't return because they don't like the strong smell. —*Susan Paige White*
North Canton, Ohio

A 5-gallon bucket hangs upside down below my bird feeder. The squirrels tried to get to my feeder (at right) for a while, but they finally gave up because they could

not get past the deep and wide bucket. —*Karen Stelling*
Bloomfield, Nebraska

If squirrels are feasting on your tulips, place chicken wire over the bulbs. The flowers will grow between the wires. —*Zelda Tedford*
Peterborough, Ontario

To keep hanging feeders squirrel-free, string a wire between two trees, drill a hole in the bottom of at least a dozen 2-liter soft-drink bottles and slide them onto the wire (below). My husband hangs several feeders and suet cages between bottles, and they have been squirrel-free since. The squirrels can't cross the bottles because they freely spin on the wire.
—*Kathryn Kelly, Aurora, Ohio*

A hanging birdbath makes a great feeder. Instead of water, I fill it with birdseed. To keep squirrels away, cut a piece of hardware cloth slightly larger than the hanging feeder. Bend the wire mesh over the sides of the dish so it's secure.

—Jill McKee-Kelso
Chula Vista, California

Trying to outwit the squirrels has not worked for me. So I keep them out of my bird feeders by giving them their own feeder. It's a simple window screen stretched over a 1-foot-high wooden frame. Now it appears all my backyard wildlife is happy. *—Carol Greene*
Wyoming, Rhode Island

I replaced my squirrel baffle with a 1-gallon milk jug. Since then, no squirrels have made it up my shepherd's hook.

—Elaine Emery Bilbruck
Carlinville, Illinois

Place thorny clippings at the base of bird feeders. Squirrels will try to cross once, but only once. They'll quickly learn to leave your feeder alone.

—Charlotte Hutcheson
Gainesville, Georgia

An empty 3-gallon plastic flowerpot makes a great baffle. Just cut a hole in the bottom of the container that's slightly wider than the feeder pole. Slide it upside down onto the pole about 1 foot below the feeder and hold it in place with a hose clamp. I've painted it so that it blends in with the background.

—Gary Schauf
Gulf Breeze, Florida

Tumbleweed is plentiful in our area. So we gather the prickly masses and position them at the base of our feeders. When it's stacked a couple of feet high, the squirrels won't climb on it. If you don't have tumbleweed in your area, use thorny branches from trees or shrubs.

—The Carmelite Sisters
Colorado Springs, Colorado

My husband nailed metal sheeting to the roof of our gazebo bird feeder (below). He extended the metal so it's almost even with the feeder platform. This allows smaller birds to fly under it to get to the seed, but keeps squirrels and larger birds out. *—Lynda Carr*
Harrodsburg, Kentucky

Smear baby oil on your metal feeder pole from the top to the bottom to keep the squirrels off. It'll need to be reapplied after heavy rains, but it works great.

—Esther Beerer, Elkhart, Indiana

Squirrels steer clear of my bird feeder after I rub crushed hot pepper on the pole. They can't stand the stuff. Wear gloves when applying and avoid touching your face or skin. *—Linda Babb*
Boyertown, Pennsylvania

I attached a bunch of aluminum pie plates to the posts that support my large bird feeder (left). My trick seems to have foiled the persistent squirrels—they don't even go near it.

—Michael Oldfield
Vancouver,
British Columbia

Morning glories climb up the base of my bird feeder. Besides looking beautiful, they also keep squirrels from climbing it as well. Plus, they attract hummingbirds.

—Carol Ann Reimer
McHenry, Illinois

> ### IT'S A FACT...
>
> There are more than 300 different kinds of squirrels throughout the world, making them one of the largest families of rodents. However, there are only six kinds of tree squirrels in North America—eastern and western gray, fox, red, tasseleared and flying squirrels. There are also many ground squirrels, which include chipmunks, marmots and prairie dogs.

If squirrels are a problem in your backyard, purchase feeders that hang from suction cups and place them in the center of a large picture window or patio door. So far, these furry critters haven't been able to get a foothold on the glass. *—Lisa Scott*
Bloomington, Indiana

Mount a metal garbage can upside down on a feeder pole. The squirrels can climb up the pole and into the garbage can, but that's as far as they get. It's fun to watch! We painted ours so it's not so obtrusive. *—Sally Schofield*
Port Richey, Florida

> ***By George...*** Although squirrels are fond of almost everything that's offered in bird feeders, safflower, niger and pure suet seem to be the exceptions.
>
> If suet cakes contain other ingredients, such as seed or fruit, squirrels will eat them.
>
> *—George Harrison, Contributing Editor*
>
> Source: Squirrel Wars

ASK GEORGE

I've resorted to using Havahart live traps, which are a humane way to remove squirrels from my yard. How far should we travel to release these critters so that they do not return?

—Thom Bird
Belcher, Louisiana

George: The most important part of the live trapping process is to transport the prisoner as many miles away as possible, so that it cannot return to the scene of the crime.

This process works well if there are only two squirrels in the neighborhood. Often, however, there are enough squirrels in the area, so that as soon as one is removed, another moves in to take its place.

Squirrels are protected by law in most states. Check with your state wildlife agency before trapping and transporting squirrels.

Wrap a thin piece of Plexiglas around your feeder posts. Squirrels can't get a foothold on it, and it looks good—it's practically invisible.

—Lorri and Dennis Schmick
Lancaster, Pennsylvania

Squirrels were chewing on my birdhouses and feeders, so I painted them. Since then, the squirrels haven't touched them.

—Joann Polgar
Abita Springs, Louisiana

I keep the squirrels from eating my birdseed by installing an aluminum cone below each feeder. I begin with a 2-foot sheet of aluminum. Cut a large circle from the sheet, then cut a straight line from the outer edge to the center of the circle. Cut a hole in the center to use around a feeder pole. Overlap the edges to make a cone. Drill holes through the overlap and secure with pop rivets or sheet metal screws. It also works well when placed above hanging feeders. *—Burton Tiffany*
Aiken, South Carolina

I've secured a funnel-shaped squirrel baffle below my feeders and another above them (below). The one on top is supported by a spring and tips easily when disturbed. These have proven to be so successful, I've even placed some of these feeders beneath trees, yet no squirrel has successfully gotten onto them.

—Jay Joyner
Durham,
North Carolina

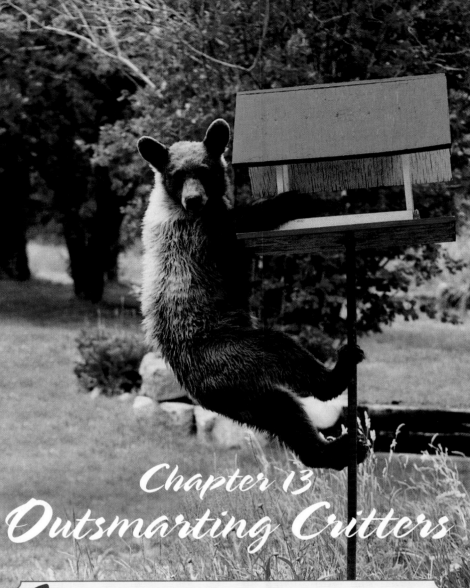

Chapter 13
Outsmarting Critters

*S*tarlings, raccoons and bears, oh my! What avid backyard birder hasn't had to deal with these pesky critters? From "bully birds" that dominate bird feeders to four-footed raiders bound and determined to steal birdseed…it's enough to make your head spin!

Luckily, readers have come up with plenty of homegrown ideas to outwit these backyard bandits. And you won't believe how *easy* some of these solutions are. So read on to discover how you, too, can create a haven that's *just* for the birds.

Photo: Robert Walton

A red-headed woodpecker used to wake me up each morning by loudly pecking on the side of my house.

To solve the problem, I mounted a plastic woodpecker decoy near its favorite spot. It fooled the noisy fellow into thinking he was too late to protect his territory. Soon, he disappeared to find a more favorable domain. —*Linda Steider*
Venetia, Pennsylvania

"Bully birds" were often raiding our platform feeder and chasing away smaller songbirds, so I devised an inexpensive and easy fix. I placed an overturned plastic storage crate

on top of the feeder and secured it with wire. Then I covered the top with a plastic lid (anything flat and waterproof will do), using a brick to keep it from blowing away.

Small birds, like black-capped chickadees, house finches, dark-eyed juncos and American goldfinches (above), can get to the food inside the crate, but larger birds are left on the outside looking in.
—*Dan Malone*
McMinnville, Tennessee

I've come up with a way to keep blue jays and squirrels occupied so other birds can dine in peace.

Denise Francisco

I buy inexpensive dry dog food and offer it in a separate feeder (like the one above). The squirrels and jays love this treat and don't touch the more expensive birdseed.

As long as I don't run out of dog food, I know my bird feeders will stay full much longer.
—*Allegra Milano*
Burlington, Maine

Birds won't wait for my sunflowers to fully ripen, so I place old pantyhose over the seed heads to protect them. Besides providing cover for the ripening seeds, the hanging "legs" wave in the breeze and discourage my feathered friends from snacking before the seeds are ready. —*B.E. Seaman*
Yellville, Arkansas

To quiet a northern mockingbird that sings at night, place a plastic model of an owl near the mockingbird's favorite perch and move it occasionally. Owls are predators, and most birds will avoid them.
—*Lorrie Evans*
Scottville, Michigan

My husband and I live just outside Shenandoah National Park, where we have to deal with bears. After numerous attempts to stop them from eating our birdseed, we found only one reliable way to protect our feeders—bring them indoors at night. It's a hassle, but it beats replacing damaged feeders.

—*Margaret Smith*
Sperryville, Virginia

When I first discovered a small black bear emptying my feeders—and destroying them in the process—I started bringing them indoors for the night. But the bear soon figured out my scheme and began visiting the feeders earlier in the day.

Next, I tried hanging my feeders on pulleys from a high tree branch. But the bear simply climbed up and used the limb as a place to relax as it feasted on the goodies.

Finally, I realized the bear could only climb large trees with few obstructing branches. So I found a smaller tree with lots of thin branches and hung the feeders well out of its reach. Now the bear doesn't bother my feeders anymore.

—*Vivian Vican*
Claryville, New York

Critters no longer raid my nest boxes since I discovered this simple solution. I wrap a heavy sheet of plastic around the birdhouse post. Cats and raccoons can't climb the slippery surface.

—*Delores McHardie*
Andrews, Indiana

By generously sprinkling chili powder on my birdseed, I no longer have to worry about raccoons raiding my feeders. Plus, I've found cats stay away, too!   —*Amelia Paulson*
Salt Lake City, Utah

To protect a low-nesting family of brown creepers from my outdoor cats, I placed chicken wire flat on the ground around the nest, leaving several large humps in it. The cats won't walk on the wire.

—*Sue Creasy*
South Mills, North Carolina

ASK GEORGE
Other than using baffles, is there a way to keep snakes from raiding my birdhouses?
—*Lysbeth Ferriola*
Woodbine, New Jersey

George: Although snakes aren't major predators of songbirds in much of the United States, squirrel baffles located above and below a birdhouse should stop them. Otherwise, you can prevent snakes from climbing by mounting birdhouses on smooth, round posts made of metal or PVC pipe. Snakes have a difficult time climbing these slippery surfaces.

Our daughter keeps cats away from her low-nesting birds by wrapping a spiked dog collar around the trunk of the tree.
—*Beverly Warburton*
Fallbrook, California

I surround my feeders with a 4-foot-tall chicken wire fence to protect the birds from cats. The fence is secured with several metal garden stakes, but is still floppy enough that cats can't climb it. There's also no ledge for them to leap to. I've found this solution works well. Plus, the thin wire doesn't detract from my view of the birds.
—*Lisa McCune-Leduc*
Belchertown, Massachusetts

Keep cats away from your bird feeder by setting a wide pile of dry pinecones at its base. Cats won't walk over the sharp cones. I dig a shallow trench around my feeder first to help keep the pinecones in place. —*Debby Roberts*
Chambersburg, Pennsylvania

> *By George…* To keep blackbirds and European starlings from eating your suet, try hanging it beneath a squirrel baffle. These birds are uncomfortable if they have to hang while eating.
> —*George Harrison*
> *Contributing*
> *Editor*

To keep cats from raiding my birdhouses, I wrap plastic bubble wrap around the base of the trees and secure it with tape. For some reason, they won't go near the stuff. Once nesting season is over, I simply remove the wrapping.
—*Becky Prigge, Napoleon, Ohio*

If you can't beat 'em, feed 'em! I put out leftover popcorn for the grackles and crows. They'll leave my bird feeders alone when I serve this treat. —*Ramona Ruhf*
Bethlehem, Pennsylvania

Stop cats from scaling trees that hold birdhouses by wrapping aluminum roofing around the base of the trees. The would-be raiders will slide right down the slick aluminum surface. Once nesting season is over, remove the roofing so the tree can grow. —*Dudley Mays*
Nashville, Tennessee

Neighborhood cats don't bother our bird feeder since we placed a pile of prickly branches at the feeder's base. Clippings from our rosebush and firethorn make the area inhospitable for these predators, while providing protection for ground-feeding birds.
—*Dora Fleming, Winder, Georgia*

Hawks don't stalk the birds at our feeders since we placed a plastic crow decoy on a nearby tree branch. We got the idea after watching the crows chase hawks as they're flying.
—*Tom and Susan Kirk*
Nazareth, Pennsylvania

hen I adopted a cat, I became
ncerned that she was attacking the
rds at my feeder. So with the help
my handy neighbor, Gary, we cre-
ed a "kitty shield" from a piece of
avy-duty hardware cloth and at-
ched it to the bottom of the feeder
ee photo above).

Once winter rolls around, we'll
ve to add a wooden frame to sup-
ort the added weight of snow. But
r now, it works like a dream.
—*Bonnie Peters-Mutzabaugh*
Dover, Pennsylvania

My neighbor gave me an idea
that's helped keep crows from roosting in my backyard. I simply played
a cassette tape of owl calls for a
few consecutive nights. Now my
yard is crow-free.   —*Ella Hunted*
Fairfield, California

Attach hardware cloth to the
roof of your covered platform feeder, so it hangs down several inches.
This will discourage crows from eating at your feeder because they're
too large to fly below it.
—*John Anderson*
Riverwoods, Illinois

Crows used to eat our sweet corn
as soon as the plants came up. So a
friend suggested we crisscross
pieces of white string over the entire
area. Since we put up this garden

barrier, we haven't had a single crow
raid our vegetable patch.
—*Barbara Taylor*
Franklinton, Louisiana

Keep house sparrows from taking over bluebird houses by placing
the nest boxes in open areas, away
from buildings. Sparrows generally
nest close to such structures, but
bluebirds prefer open terrain.
—*Bud Sickler*
Leesburg, Florida

Tape the entrances of your bluebird nest boxes shut to keep house
sparrows out. Remove the tape once
bluebirds arrive.   —*Jesse Swarey*
Belleville, Pennsylvania

Ever since we mounted our bird
feeders on poles made of 3-inch
PVC plumbing pipe, we haven't had
problems with raccoons raiding our
birdseed. It works for squirrels, too.
—*Carol Brewer*
Boonville, Missouri

Protect your suet
from crows by serv-
ing it in a wire mesh
peanut feeder. The
openings are too
small for their large
bills, but woodpeck-
ers' smaller bills are
a perfect fit (right).
—*Diana Kidd*
Alexandria, Virginia

Snakes will avoid bluebird houses if you wrap their mounting posts
with aluminum foil.   —*Susie King*
Holtwood, Pennsylvania

Ants used to target our hummingbird feeders, but my husband outsmarted them.  He ran the wire hanger of the feeder through a small hole in the bottom of a clean tuna can (left) and sealed the hole with some silicon. (The caps of spray-paint cans and laundry detergent bottles work well, too). Then he filled the can with 1/2 inch of water.

The first ant that reached the water turned back. It must have spread the word because I haven't seen another one since. —*Thelma Rhicard Stanbridge East, Quebec*

It's a challenge preventing house sparrows from nesting in my bluebird houses, but I've realized persistence has its rewards.

I clean the houses in mid-winter and close them up (seal the entrance with tape, a large cork, etc.) to keep sparrows from roosting in them. When bluebirds show interest in the boxes in spring, I reopen them.

If a sparrow inhabits the box, I clean out the nest (house sparrows' nests are not protected by federal law because they're not native birds), close the entrance again and wait until a bluebird stops by before reopening it.

This process takes time, but when I see young bluebirds emerge from the houses, I know the extra work was definitely worthwhile.

—*Sheila Blanchard Falkville, Alabama*

Sparrows don't even try to build nests in my bluebird house anymore since I started using an open-top design. The screened top keeps sparrows out because they won't nest in an open cavity. Bluebirds don't seem to mind, however. And once the beautiful birds establish a nest, I add a temporary roof to shield them from the elements.

—*Linda Rinck, Pittsford, Michigan*

Keep ants out of hummingbird feeders by hanging them from copper wire. (We buy the insulated kind and remove the plastic insulation). The wire contains elements that are harmful to ants, but are perfectly safe for birds. We've successfully used this technique for 18 years.

—*Betty Steadman, Baker, Nevada*

Ants stay away from my hummingbird feeder since I began using this method. I cut out a 2-inch square of cloth, dip it in cooking oil and slide it onto the feeder's wire hanger. Then I rub a bit of oil on the wire. The feeder stays ant-free all summer. —*Pearl Robertson San Angelo, Texas*

> ### IT'S A FACT...
> Keep "bully birds" off your feeders by offering safflower seed. Crows, European starlings and pigeons generally won't eat it, but most smaller songbirds will.

Keep ants from hummingbird feeders with an item that's made to protect houseplants from pests. It's called "sticky stake". We cut a small disk from the stake, poke a hole in it and slide it onto the wire that holds the feeder. After a few dozen ants got stuck on the disk, we didn't have any more ant problems.
—*Dick and June Luerssen Baldwin, Maryland*

I place double-sided tape around the string from which my hummingbird feeder hangs. The tape isn't sticky enough to bother birds, but it does deter ants!
—*Georgia McWomary Thornton, New Hampshire*

Apply a thin layer of Avon Skin-So-Soft bath oil to the wire that holds a hummingbird feeder and around the feeding ports. Ants and bees won't attempt to steal the sweet nectar anymore.   —*Ann Fries Wolcottville, Indiana*

Keep ants out of sugar-water feeders by generously sprinkling cinnamon on top of the feeder.
—*Sarah Fitting Grass Valley, California*

Stop ants from invading hummingbird feeders by applying nonstick cooking spray or a thin coat of solid shortening to the feeder's hanger. Ants can't stand it!
—*Mary Blodgett St. Charles, Missouri*

Common grackles were a problem at my feeder, until I removed the perches and added a "tail board". The board allows woodpeckers to prop themselves up as they feed (above right), yet it keeps the grackles from feeding (above left).
—*Edward Thompson, Miami, Florida*

My father, Paul, devised a way to keep ants out of his hummingbird feeders. He placed a small wooden dowel through a plastic funnel so it stuck out about 6 inches on either side. Then he attached screw eyes on both ends of the dowel.

To hold the funnel in place and keep it from leaking, he applied a bit of silicone around the dowel at the funnel's base. The final step was filling the funnel with a little water. It works like a charm!
—*Charles Kunze Sr. Chesterville, Ohio*

We use mineral oil to keep ants, wasps and bees from invading our hummingbird and oriole feeders. We just rub the oil on the feeding ports after we clean them and add a little to the feeder's hanger, too.
—*Marian Bauerle Marana, Arizona*

I found a way to stop ants from getting caught in our hummingbird feeder, plus provide an additional water source for small birds like goldfinches.

Cut off the top several inches of a 2-liter soft drink bottle and drill a small hole in the bottle cap. Slip a sturdy wire through the hole and bend both ends into hooks. Seal the hole with a little caulk. After it dries, fill the basin with water and hang the homemade ant trap between the hummingbird feeder and its hook.

—*Marilyn Ziegelmeyer*
Covington, Kentucky

Although my bird feeder (above) has a weight-sensitive bar that shuts when critters heavier than birds sit on it, a few have figured out how to hang from the roof and eat without touching it. So I attached an old refrigerator rack to its roof. The rack is a several inches longer and wider than the roof, which is enough to foil the furry raiders.

—*Jerold Dalton*
Brookfield, Wisconsin

Wasps constantly invaded our sugar-water feeder, until I created some homemade "bee guards". I cut out circles of plastic mesh and pushed them into the feeding ports.

Now wasps can't reach the nectar, but hummingbirds still have access.

—*Norma Poettgen*
Kennedale, Texas

To keep bees away from my sugar-water feeders, I rub a little liquid smoke around the feeding ports.

—*Jacob Miller*
Chaseburg, Wisconsin

I apply a little petroleum jelly to the shepherd's hook that holds my hummingbird feeder. This keeps ants out of the feeder, reserving the sugar water for hummingbirds.

—*Nancy Holden*
Disputanta, Virginia

I accidentally discovered this solution for keeping wasps from my hummingbird feeders. I placed a new oriole feeder—which has large open feeding ports—on the shepherd's hook next to my hummingbird feeder. Wasps now choose the easy-access oriole feeder over the smaller ports of the hummingbird feeder.

The Baltimore orioles aren't scared of these insects the way the hummingbirds are, so they have no problem using their feeder. And the hummers enjoy wasp-free dining.

—*Bonita Laettner*
Angola, New York

Insects like wasps and hornets don't harass birds in our backyard haven because I have a tried-and-true way to trap them. Here's how:

In a clean 2-liter soft drink bottle, mix 1/2 cup vinegar with 1 cup sugar, then fill it with water to about 2 inches below the bottle's neck. Cut a banana peel into strips and drop the pieces into the bottle. Cover and shake until the sugar is dissolved. Now place or hang the uncapped bottle in your backyard.

Hornets and wasps are attracted to the fermenting fruit, but get stuck in the sugary concoction. When the bottle has done its job, just throw it away and set out a new one.
—*Kathy Miller*
Waukesha, Wisconsin

Hornets and wasps often are a problem in bird and bat houses. But you can prevent them from taking over by painting a few thin layers of petroleum jelly on the underside of the roof. The insects won't be able to attach their paper nests to the slick surface. —*Sandra Sullivan*
Oak Brook, Illinois

Like many birders, we rub petroleum jelly on our feeder poles to keep critters from climbing them. To make it even more effective, we mix Tabasco sauce into the jelly!

Once the raiders get a taste of the spicy substance, they're not so eager to return for seconds.
—*Mary Oheim*
Springfield, Missouri

My tube feeders are reserved for American goldfinches, black-

capped chickadees, downy woodpeckers and white-breasted nuthatches. That's because I cut the perches so they're only about 3/4 inch long. Birds like house sparrows and house finches can't perch on them anymore. —*Carol Boynton*
Dixon, Illinois

My neighbor, Margaret Whittlesey, was upset when pigeons began taking over her tray feeder. Her hus-

band, Max, eliminated the problem by constructing a protective screen cover (above). He used scrap lumber and enclosed the tray feeder with wire fencing with 2- x 3-inch spaces.

It works perfectly. The screen keeps large birds out, while allowing small songbirds to feed in peace.
—*Colleen Slater*
Vaughn, Washington

After an egret took a liking to the koi in my backyard pond, I stretched some fine netting above the water's surface. Although this stopped the egret, it also stranded the frogs.

Then someone suggested I add a great blue heron decoy. I found one at local garden supply store and haven't had a problem with the egret since. —*Barbara Casteen*
Wilmington, North Carolina

IT'S A FACT...
House sparrows were introduced to North America in 1850 in New York's Central Park. They're natives of Europe.

Each night, hundreds of house sparrows roosted in the large elm tree in our backyard. Not only were they noisy, but they created quite a mess.

A relative suggested we spray the birds with water to scare them away. It worked!

We sprayed the enormous flock every night for a week with a power washer that could reach the high branches. The flock dwindled each night and eventually stopped coming altogether. —*Midge Hudak Highland, Indiana*

When a blue jay started attacking the nesting house finches (below) in my yard, I had to do some-

thing to protect them. So I went to the store and purchased a badminton net, which I carefully wrapped around the potted begonia where the nest was hidden. The holes in the netting were about 1-1/2 inches square—large enough for the finches to enter and exit, but too small for the jay. —*Diane Pravecek Lawrence, Kansas*

My mugo pine provided great protective cover for birds at my hanging feeders, until a persistent northern

IT'S A FACT...
A squirrel's average life span is 1 year. Only about 25% will live longer than that.

harrier discovered their hiding place. It began following them into the tree!

To save the small birds, I placed pieces of green-coated wire fencing with 2- x 4-inch holes in the tree. I cut the fencing into manageable sizes that could be arranged among the branches. It's barely visible.

Smaller birds can easily fit through the fencing, but that northern harrier is stuck on the outside. —*Nanci Stankus North Smithfield, Rhode Island*

Seagulls are plentiful near our condo in Ocean City, Maryland. One bothersome behavior we've noticed is the birds often drop shellfish onto area roofs to crack open the shells. It creates a mess and sometimes even damages the houses.

Some residents began using painted seagull decoys to trick the birds into thinking one of their relatives was waiting to steal the catch. Most of the time, seagulls fly to a different destination to protect their meal. —*Jim Prow Baltimore, Maryland*

Suspend your tray feeder from a clothesline by attaching a wire hanger to each end of the feeder. The gentle swinging and wobbly clothesline will keep most feeder raiders away. —*Nana Flesch Belmont, Wisconsin*

Keep snakes out of birdhouses by sprinkling a few bay leaves at the base of the post or tree that supports it. —*Henry Delagrange Sr.*
Montgomery, Michigan

To stop raccoons from raiding our bird feeder, I greased the metal pole and added a little cayenne pepper to the grease. I haven't seen a raccoon near the feeder since.
—*Noella Cormier*
St. Paul, New Brunswick

House sparrows steer clear of my purple martin house since I rigged up a system to scare them.

I tied a lead sinker to a long thin piece of string, then threaded it through a screw eye attached at the bottom of the martin house. The string extends all the way to our kitchen window and into the house through a small opening.

Whenever I see a sparrow near the house, I tug on the string, causing the sinker to tap against the house. The sudden noise sends the sparrows scurrying.
—*Owen Johnson*
Caledonia, Michigan

To protect my tube feeder from critters, I created a double-layer baffle that can't be beat. First there's a squirrel baffle hanging directly over the feeder. But the real key is a plastic 2-liter soft drink bottle that hangs directly above the baffle, creating a second barrier (above). —*Bill Reagan*
Endwell, New York

We live in the middle of Vancouver Island and have a wonderful variety of birds at our feeders. But pigeons, Steller's jays and European starlings were ransacking our backyard "restaurant".

To keep larger "bully birds" from chasing smaller ones from our tube feeder, we shortened the perches and cut off the bottom plate so they would no longer be able to land and eat. Now we enjoy watching the smaller birds feed in peace again.
—*Sally Anderson*
Port Alberni, British Columbia

Save your thistle seed from European starlings with my easy technique. Purchase two large plastic colanders and cut a hole in the bottom of each one—the holes should be large enough for your tube feeder to fit through. Then slide the colanders onto your feeder to create a protected enclosure. Leave an opening between them that's large enough for finches to enter. Then connect the handles with wire (see photo at left).

An added bonus is that the colanders collect spilled seed. The birds eat that, too.
—*Ralph Hicks, Eden, North Carolina*

European starlings can't feed at my suet cage since I placed a roof over it. I created the simple pitched roof with two scrap boards. By drilling a hole in the center of the roof, I was able to easily thread the suet cage hanger through the roof and suspend it from a tree branch. The starlings can't get a good grip on the feeder in the new cramped quarters.　　　—D. Cecil Smith
Germantown, Ohio

Keep raccoons from raiding your suet feeder by hanging it from the tip of a branch that won't support the weight of the larger animals. Make sure you hang it high enough so squirrels can't jump to it from the ground.　　　—John Dee Garrick
Grove Hill, Alabama

To prevent predatory birds from attacking the finches at our thistle seed feeder, we built a protective cage around it. We used plastic flats from the local nursery and some string to create a box-like structure. The holes in the flats are large enough for finches to fly through, but large birds can't squeeze in.
　　　—*Marvin and
Twyla Sorensen
Salida, Colorado*

I thought I'd have to stop feeding birds after four hawks started frequenting our backyard. But after I removed the feeders, woodpeckers, finches, doves and cardinals kept coming back, looking for their food. So I decided to make a scarecrow from an old broom.

I stuck the handle in the ground, put a bright hat on its bristles and wrapped a piece of cloth around it like a cape. The songbirds don't mind the new visitor, but the hawks haven't returned.　　　—*Jean Hauck
Fountain Hills, Arizona*

After I noticed northern cardinals usually eat early and late in the day, I started waiting until late afternoon to put out sunflower seed. By then, the grackles, cowbirds, redwinged blackbirds and starlings that used to raid my bird feeders have given up.

Birds like cardinals and Harris's sparrows now dine in peace. And if

We keep black-billed magpies (top right) from eating our birdseed by providing a feeding station just for them. I place pieces of suet on a stump, far away from my other feeders, then cover it with chicken wire (bottom right). This keeps the greedy birds from taking all the suet at once.

I also offer inexpensive dry dog food on a platform feeder. With two feeding options to choose from, the magpies leave the birdseed alone.
　　　—*Deck Hunter
Big Horn, Wyoming*

they eat all the seed, I replenish the feeder early the next morning—but only with the amount they'll eat in one sitting. —*Jo Ann Sheldon Arkansas City, Kansas*

I live on an island in the St. Lawrence River, where we see a lot of Canada geese. Although we love watching these beautiful birds, they create quite a mess when they venture onto our lawn and driveway.

To keep the birds at a distance, we placed several wooden stakes 10 to 15 feet apart at the shoreline and ran string between them. For whatever reason, the geese won't cross these barriers and remain in the river instead. —*Velda Schlyer Wellesley Island, New York*

We have several tray feeders mounted to a wooden fence. The setup worked fine until a stray cat started lurking around. To protect the birds, we installed wire fencing with 2- x 4-inch openings above the feeder, angling it toward the ground. The birds can still easily access the feeders, but the cat can no longer jump to them. —*Kelly Smith Wichita, Kansas*

I purchased a couple upside-down suet cages for my woodpeckers, but crafty European starlings soon realized they could hang on to the wire long enough to nibble or dislodge some suet. So I tied several 6-inch pieces of thin nylon string to the underside of the wire cage. The dangling strings distract the starlings' balance just enough so they can't steal suet. —*Carolyn Lathrop Dixon, Illinois*

To keep critters away from my birdseed, I enclosed the feeders in a metal cage—the kind we use around

here to catch Maryland blue crabs. This allows small birds to eat peacefully inside the cage, while raccoons and squirrels are out of luck (see photo above). —*Belva Barbalace Grasonville, Maryland*

Grackles, crows, blackbirds and other "bully birds" have stopped visiting my yard because I quit offering table scraps, removed all the suet and put out only niger (thistle) for the finches and safflower seed for the cardinals, chickadees and nuthatches. —*S. Lynn Cartee Bessemer, Alabama*

Attach 1/2-inch hardware cloth over the openings of hopper feeders. Birds can reach through the mesh with their bills, but raccoons and squirrels can't. —*Dan Miller Longmont, Colorado*

A chain-link enclosure that used to be a dog kennel is now a safe haven for backyard birds. We hang our feeders in this protected area and no longer worry about cats catching our feathered friends.

We even placed a birdbath in the enclosure, which is close enough to our house to provide a great bird-watching display. —*Carol Richards Holly, Michigan*

My husband built this heavy-duty feeder (above) to keep grackles, blue jays and other large birds from taking over. The cage's largest openings are 1-3/4 inches wide, allowing only small birds access.

So far, the feeder has been a resounding success. It attracts all sorts of finches, chickadees, nuthatches and sparrows, yet keeps the larger ones from the feeders. It's also proven to be squirrel-proof! —*Lee Donald Caledon Village, Ontario*

I surrounded my wrought-iron plant hanger with 3-inch PVC plumbing pipe and suspended feeders from its hooks. To make it blend in with my rosebush, I stenciled pink roses on the pipe and then protected the design with a coat of clear varnish. The feeder not only foils potential raiders, but makes a pretty garden accent, too.

—*Mary Dahlgren Maple Lake, Minnesota*

We have a squirrel-proof feeder that's triggered by a weight-sensitive perch. If a squirrel or large bird lands on the perch, the feeding trough closes.

This feeder worked fine, until raccoons somehow figured out a way around it. So we came up with a solution. We fill an aluminum can with stones and hang it from the perch each night. This keeps the feeder firmly closed until we remove the can in the morning. —*Judy Recher Hopewell, Virginia*

European starlings were trying to set up housekeeping in my birdhouses by enlarging the entrance holes. To stop them, I placed a short piece of plastic PVC pipe on the inside of each entrance hole, securing it with caulk. After the starlings realized they couldn't enlarge the for-

tified openings, they left to search for more inviting nesting sites.
—*Mary Sieber*
East Quogue, New York

Stop European starlings and grackles from stealing your suet by cutting the bottom off a 1-gallon milk jug and suspending the jug over your suet cage. Woodpeckers have no problem eating under this domed roof, but starlings and grackles can't hang and feed.
—*Leslie Oswald*
Cherry Valley, Illinois

To stop pests from raiding my bird feeder, I put a "Slinky" around the pole and attached it to the feeder's bottom. When animals attempt to climb the pole, the stretchy toy keeps them from getting a good grip.
—*Joelle Stanoch*
Sartell, Minnesota

For years, my husband, Jim, has outwitted backyard wildlife by

hanging our bird feeders and suet trays on a 1/4-inch nylon rope suspended between our deck and a tree in our yard (above).

He simply lowers the feeders to the ground to fill them, then puts them back up when he's done. The squirrels still haven't figured it out.
—*Sandy Erickson*
Midway, Arkansas

Even though safflower seed is more expensive than sunflower seed, it costs less in the end because greedy grackles avoid it. The squirrels don't like it either.
—*Stan Merrill, Kokomo, Indiana*

ASK GEORGE
I'd appreciate any suggestions about keeping sparrows out of my bluebird houses.
—*Ginnie Bowling, Lawton, Michigan*

George: You can discourage sparrows from using bluebird houses by locating the houses at the edges of open fields. That's where the habitat is more suitable to bluebirds than house sparrows.

Make sure the entrance holes are no larger than 1-1/2 inches in diameter for eastern bluebird houses, and 1-9/16 inches for mountain and western bluebirds. Also, you can legally remove house sparrows' nesting materials because they're not native North American birds.

I received lots of great advice from *Birds & Blooms* readers about how to keep house sparrows out of my tree swallow houses. Here are a couple of their suggestions:

• Don't leave the birdhouses up year-round. Put them up just before tree swallows return in spring. By then, most sparrows have already found nesting sites.

• Place nest boxes at least 125 feet from the nearest building. Sparrows will not nest that far from "civilization".
—*Marcia Lane*
Enumclaw, Washington

To prevent deer and rabbits from raiding my bird garden at night, I place an old radio nearby. Tuned to a music station, it plays just loud enough to keep the flower-munching critters at bay.
—*Edward Stern*
Fargo, North Dakota

ASK GEORGE
How can I prevent wasps from building nests in my birdhouses?
—*Wendy Creasy*
Gassville, Arkansas

George: You can keep wasps out of your birdhouses by plugging the entrance holes until birds are ready to use them in spring. The wasps won't invade the houses once they're occupied—the birds will see to that.

After the birds move on, either take down the houses or plug the holes again.

You also could try hanging a wasp trap in the general area of the birdhouse, but not right next to it.

How can I keep wasps and yellow jackets away from my hummingbird feeders? —*Catherine Adams*
Riverdale, Maryland

George: Wasp and bee traps, baited with sugar water and placed relatively near your feeders, should reduce the number of wasps and bees. You can also discourage insects by treating the outside of the feeder ports with Vicks VapoRub (or any petroleum-based menthol rub) or Avon's Skin-So-Soft.

I am looking for some advice about how to keep hawks away from my backyard birds.
—*Marcelia Suter*
Harrisonburg, Virginia

George: The best way to protect songbirds from hawks in your backyard is to provide sufficient cover—brush, shrubs and trees. Then smaller birds will have a protective place they can escape into if attacked. Because federal law protects hawks, they cannot be trapped or harmed in any way.

Chapter 14
Odds & Ends

Birds & Blooms readers sent in so many unique and interesting tips for this book that we couldn't find a place for them all in the previous chapters. So here, we've gathered a mixed flock of birding secrets that didn't seem to fit anywhere else...but were simply too good to pass up.

On the following pages, you'll find plenty of ways to make backyard bird-watching more enjoyable, whether it's creating a handy and inexpensive seed scoop or discovering how to bring the sounds of songbirds inside. There are even ideas on how to get your kids interested in *your* favorite hobby.

Make backyard bird-watching more fun by keeping a "backyard bird list" of the different species you've spotted from your house. We've recorded 72 species over the years. —*Pamela Conley Cazadero, California*

Many birds dust bathe to keep their feathers healthy. I built a four-walled dust bath from scrap boards (like the one below), filling it with dry sand and a little ash from my fireplace. I placed it on the ground near protective cover so birds are safe while keeping clean.
—*Jon Forman, Norman, Oklahoma*

Richard Day/Daybreak Imagery

When the perches fell out of my tube feeders, I replaced them with ballpoint pen caps. The caps fit perfectly inside the holes. —*Donna Lee Rushville, Indiana*

A pair of American robins built their nest right outside our window one spring. Although they were a joy to watch, they constantly fought their reflections in the glass. So I applied a thick coat of glass wax to the window, leaving several "peep holes" so we could still see the young robins. The wax obscured the birds' reflections enough to stop the problem. Once they left, we wiped our window clean.
—*Imogene Schaefer Tulsa, Oklahoma*

I store birdseed in clean 1-gallon milk jugs. The jugs keep the seed safe from critters and make refilling feeders a breeze.
—*Ruth Turpin, Hamilton, Ohio*

A recycled mesh onion bag makes a simple and inexpensive suet feeder. —*Will Griffin Vestaburg, Michigan*

To prevent birds from flying into our patio door, we place an oscillating fan just inside of it. The fan's constant movement keeps birds away. —*Raymond Lundry Mesa, Arizona*

Set a tall round tomato cage in a large flower pot for year-round bird-watching opportunities. I often see hummingbirds perched on the cage, waiting for a turn at the sugar-water feeders or birdbath.

I plant some alyssum in the container and let it go to seed. The next spring, many birds use pieces of it to build their nests.
—*Juanita Stinchfield Hagerstown, Maryland*

IT'S A FACT... In 1940, scientist W.R. Van Dersal studied the feeding habits of wildlife and discovered more than 94 North American bird species eat acorns.

By George... If you're looking for good bird-watching binoculars, consider two main factors: magnification and sharpness of the images. There are two numbers that describe these capabilities.

The first number is the power of magnification. For example, a bird viewed through 7 x 35 binoculars is magnified seven times. The second number is the diameter, in millimeters, of the front lens. Larger lenses gather more light, making the image you see clearer and brighter.

Bigger binoculars aren't nec-essarily better, however. Greater magnification and clarity require more glass, which makes binoculars heavier. And higher magnification can make it difficult to quickly spot a bird because the image is so close.

Therefore, 7 x 35 or 8 x 40 binoculars are the best choices for most birders. —*George Harrison*
Contributing Editor

We've found an easy way to install lots of birdhouses and bird feeders in our backyard. We attach them to short pieces of PVC pipe and then slip the pipe over our fence posts (see photo above).

To do this yourself, use screws to fasten a plastic PVC cap to the bottom of a feeder or birdhouse. Then secure a 6-inch length of PVC pipe inside the cap. The diameter of the pipe and cap will vary depending on the size of your fence post. —*Tim and Connie Fisher*
Winamac, Indiana

To get a good look at a screech owl, try imitating its call. These owls are quite curious and will often fly in for a closer look. I once got one of these birds to venture within 3 feet of my family and me while we were camping. —*Diane Nelson*
Schenectady, New York

A recycled 2-liter soft drink bottle makes a perfect seed scoop. Just wash it, remove the label and cut away the bottom at an angle. It costs nothing and lasts forever.

—*Eva Elder, Evansville, Indiana*

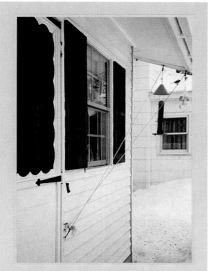

I couldn't reach my feeders to refill them, so my son created a pulley system for me.

He installed a screw eye under my eaves for each feeder and placed a small hook and eye within easy reach on the side of my house.

Then he attached a rope to the feeder and threaded it through the top screw eye. When the feeder needs refilling, I just lower the feeder. When finished, I raise it and secure the lower hook. He's taken the chore out of feeding the birds. —*Helen Clark Johannesburg, Michigan*

We use air-conditioning all summer, so our windows are seldom open. That means we can't hear birds singing. So we came up with a way to enjoy their songs in our house.

We purchased an intercom set and placed one unit outside near our trees and bird feeders, locking the talk switch in the "on" position. Then we placed the other units in our bedroom, dining room and living room so we could listen to the birds' songs throughout the house.

—*Chet and Glendine Hamilton Zellwood Station, Florida*

The birds were eating all our blackberries. So we hung a cow skull on a post in the patch. Now they avoid the berries and opt for a nearby feeder instead. —*Diane Sisk Pendleton, Oregon*

Birds seem to enjoy eating my tomatoes as much as I do. To discourage them, I hang red Christmas ornaments from the vines before the fruit ripens. The birds investigate the globes and realize they aren't edible. By the time the real tomatoes ripen, the birds aren't interested.

—*Holly Mohr, Arlington, Texas*

Hang old compact discs in berry trees to keep birds from getting to the fruit first. —*Gloria Nielsen East Olympia, Washington*

If birds are pilfering your berries, plant some of their favorites, like wild cherry, elderberry and mulberry, nearby. The fruits of these trees and shrubs will dull the birds' appetite for your favorite berries.

—*Ann Ward, Naples, Florida*

Attract tons of birds by creating a miniature bird haven in an unused corner of your yard. I planted viburnum, ornamental grasses and purple coneflowers, added a shepherd's hook with feeders, placed a birdbath nearby and removed the grass to create an area for "dirt baths". Before I knew it, I had a bird's paradise!

—*Barbara Manheim*
New Lenox, Illinois

Here's how to create unique containers to store your birdseed (below). First spray paint an old 5-gallon plastic bucket and let it dry. Then cut out photos of birds (I use photos from past *Birds & Blooms* issues) and glue them to the bucket with craft glue to make a collage.

The final step is protecting the design with several coats of water-

IT'S A FACT...
Ever wonder how many seeds are in a 50-pound bag of sunflower seed? Well, hand-counting 5 ounces of seed turns up almost 3,000 seeds. That means there are about 480,000 seeds in each 50-pound bag!

based craft varnish. The result is a critter-proof container you won't want to hide in the garage or garden shed.   —*Sue Cole, Houston, Texas*

At harvesttime, I cut down my sunflowers and remove the seed heads. Then I use the leftover stalks to create "tepees" for birds to roost in. Just gather the tops of the stalks with rope and spread the bottoms for stability.   —*Wilbur Jensen*
Onalaska, Wisconsin

When I noticed water dripping into my bird feeder from a small hole in its lid, I plugged it with some blue putty, the kind used to attach posters to walls. Now my birdseed stays dry and fresh, regardless of the weather.   —*Michelle Auch*
Waterport, New York

ASK GEORGE
Is it safe to use pressure-treated wood for building birdhouses? —Jack Player, Oswego, Illinois

George: Most pressure-treated wood contains chemicals to preserve the wood from rotting. These chemicals may be harmful to birds, and therefore, treated wood should not be used to build birdhouses.

With nine young children, there often are leftover peanut butter and jelly sandwiches after lunch. So we give the extras to the birds. We just place the pieces on a tray feeder and watch the birds finish the meal.
—*Elaine Schmit*
Mt. Pleasant Mills, Pennsylvania

Kids love this fun bird-feeding project. All you need is peanut butter, birdseed and several small milk cartons. Just cover each carton with the peanut butter and sprinkle it with birdseed. Then attach a ribbon through the top, and hang it from tree branch.
—*Kristi Salisbury*
Centreville, Virginia

To give our children an up-close look at feathered friends, my wife began placing raisins on a wooden shelf attached to our kitchen windowsill. The American robins loved this treat, and so did our kids. They could literally get nose to bill with these beautiful creatures!

When the raisins were gone, the birds would perch in a nearby tree until we replenished the supply. In spring, my wife would even cut the raisins into smaller pieces for the young birds. They'd fly to the shelf and chirp until their parents came to feed them.
—*Orville Wolff*
Daleville, Alabama

I removed the bottom of a clean bleach jug to create a sturdy seed funnel for filling my feeders (below). The handle makes it easy to hold while the spout directs the seed right where I want it.
—*Paul Emerling*
Springville, New York

Here's a winter bird-feeding project for kids. Flatten stale bread with a rolling pin, cut it into shapes with a cookie cutter, brush a beaten egg over it and press it in some birdseed. Then hang the edible decorations outside and watch feathered friends fly in to feast. —*Tina Jacobs Wantage, New Jersey*

Birds often drop their sunflower seeds in uninvited places, creating sprouts throughout our yard. Since the plants seem to grow so easily, my husband, Michael, suggested we try planting our own sunflower patch in a section of our yard where we couldn't grow healthy grass.

The results exceeded my expectations. Sunflowers of all sizes and colors now grow uninhibited in this productive patch.

I no longer need to feed our backyard birds sunflower seeds...they have a seemingly endless supply to choose from each day. —*Darlene Rokosky Thompson, Ohio*

To help bluebirds get accustomed to my enclosed mealworm feeder, I prop open the hinged top with a stick. After they've entered the box a few times through its side entrances, I remove the stick. Once they've found this reliable source of mealworms, they'll keep coming back for more. —*Patti Farnum Nashville, Michigan*

Birds stopped raiding our strawberry patch after we suspended compact discs from PVC arches above the berries (above). Since we often receive free discs in the mail, we have plenty for the garden.
—*Mrs. Arthur Garland Sr. Pembroke, Massachusetts*

ASK GEORGE
What do seed-eating birds feed their young?
—*Donna Dawley, Tustin, Michigan*

George: Seed-eating birds almost always feed insects to their young. Common backyard birds, such as northern cardinals, black-capped chickadees and blue jays, are primarily seed-eaters as adults, but feed their young high-protein food like caterpillars, spiders and flying insects.

When installing bluebird houses in an open field, face the entrance hole south, southeast or east. The dawn sunlight can warm the box on cool mornings. The hot afternoon sun could overheat the young in nest boxes that face west.

—*George Webb, Marion, Ohio*

Barbara Dunn

Keeping bluebirds satisfied with mealworms (above) from the pet store or bait shop is expensive. So I decided to "grow" my own. Here's how:

• First, buy some mealworms and place them in a large bucket or trash can on top of some cornmeal or oat bran (enough to cover the bottom to a depth of about 3 to 4 inches).

• Cut several medium-sized apples or potatoes in half and place them cut-side down on the grain. These supply moisture and should be replaced every week or so.

• Put a piece of cloth inside the container on top of the cornmeal or bran, then cover it with a lid that allows the air to circulate.

• Leave the container in a warm dark place. In about 2 or 3 weeks, the mealworms become beetles (don't worry, they rarely fly), which lay eggs on the cloth. When the pupas hatch, they burrow into the cornmeal or bran to develop before returning to the surface as mealworms.

• When they re-emerge, feed some to your bluebirds right away. Within a week or two, the rest will change into beetles and the cycle begins again.

To keep the container from becoming smelly, change the grain occasionally and sift out beetle shells. —*Linda Margo Niles, Ohio*

Bluebirds flock to the seeds of our bittersweet vine and sumac when the plants go to seed each autumn. —*Ralph and Frances Myers Greenwich, New York*

To keep birds out of my strawberry patch, I place a clock radio in my garden and set the music alarm for early morning. I put the radio in a plastic bucket that's turned on its side to protect it from dew.
—*Grace Anderson Schrunk Blaine, Minnesota*

Face bluebird houses east to attract more of these pretty birds. They should be mounted in long open fields. —*Matthew Yoder Bloomfield, Iowa*

Birds don't crash into my window now that I've placed a feeder nearby. If they do, they're too close to get hurt. —*Paul McAfee Fort Wayne, Indiana*

To keep a northern cardinal from attacking its reflection in the side mirrors of my husband's truck (and from making a mess), we placed two plastic owls in the rafters of our carport. We haven't seen the cardinal since. —*Elaine Emery Bilbruck Carlinville, Illinois*

Birds sometimes ruin my hanging flower baskets by nesting in them. So I place a fake bird (I buy mine at the fabric store) in each basket in early spring. Since I started doing this, birds no longer nest among my blooms. —*Karen Wagner Ames, Iowa*

We used to cover our berries and vegetables with netting to discourage birds. But it was a time-consuming and bothersome task. So I bought some stuffed toys from a thrift store and hung them on stakes around the plants (see photo below).

It's comical to watch birds sail in for a bite and quickly fly away when they see these animals swaying in the breeze. It works so well we now use the swinging toys everywhere in our garden, from the grape arbor to our fig tree.
—*Emmylu Lawrence Beaverton, Oregon*

Here's an easy way to keep algae from forming in your birdbath. Simply change the water in it every day. Don't forget to quickly scrub it with a brush. Then rinse and fill with fresh water. Nothing to it!
—*Pat Schuldt Sussex, Wisconsin*

We had several bird feeders in our yard, but not many winged visitors. Since there were no trees in the immediate area, we placed a wooden rack used to dry clothes nearby. I figured it would serve as a kind of protective cover and a spot for birds to perch as they check out the surroundings before landing on the feeder. As soon as we did this, we noticed an instant increase in the number of birds.

—Leslie Demargerie
Sprague, Manitoba

'Orphaned' Birds Often in Mom's Sight

Nancy Jenzano

Bird lover Tom Kovach of Park Rapids, Minnesota learned a few things about "orphaned" birds from biologist Jimmy Ernst of the Louisiana Department of Wildlife and Fisheries.

• "Some young birds leave the nest before they can fly, so don't assume something is wrong when a young bird is on the ground," Jimmy explains. "In most cases, the parents are nearby, waiting for you to leave so they can continue teaching the fledgling how to find food or fend for itself."

• "If it's obvious a young bird has fallen from its nest, and predators, like house cats, are a concern, put it back in the nest or place it on a branch," Jimmy says.

"If the parent doesn't return after several hours, there may be a certified wildlife rehabilitator in your area who can provide for the youngster."

• "No one other than a certified wildlife rehabilitator should try to care for baby birds," Jimmy says. "Most people have no idea what to feed young birds and could give them food that's unsuitable or harmful." (And besides, federal law prohibits keeping native songbirds captive without a proper license.)

"Birds tend to draw human sympathy," Jimmy notes. "But what first appears to be a tragedy is probably a completely normal situation."

My nest boxes are more successful since I added a 3-inch-long wooden extension around each entrance hole. Build a small square box from scrap wood (leave ends open) and attach it around the entrance to keep predators out.

—*George Schneider*
Liberty, Illinois

Collect the fruits of mountain ash trees in autumn. I keep them in the refrigerator until winter, then take some outside and hold them in my open hands. Usually, I don't have to wait long for the Bohemian waxwings to eat from my hands. It's a lot of fun. —*Robert Morin*
Lac-Saint-Charles, Quebec

Keep predators out of your bluebird nest boxes by mounting the boxes on tall pieces of steel pipe. I use an 8-1/2-foot length of pipe and bury it about 2-1/2 feet in the ground. Then I drill a hole near the top of the pipe for a bolt to attach the nest box. The bottom of the box should be 5 feet off the ground.

—*George Webb, Marion, Ohio*

When a tree limb fell into the area I designated as our bird sanctuary, I decided to use the opportunity to create a protective hedgerow. I hauled in other downed limbs and small twigs I'd gathered after storms and added them to the pile.

Now this area offers birds shelter from weather and predators. I've also placed two platform feeders, a suet cage and several other feeders nearby. —*Joan Heinle*
Whiting, Iowa

Make finch feeders from plastic poster tubes. I cut them to 14 inches long, poke a tiny feeding hole about 4 inches from the bottom, and drill a larger hole through the entire tube a couple inches below it.

Insert a wooden dowel into the large hole as a perch and cap both ends of the tube. Your feeder is complete. I attract lots of finches, like this American gold-finch (above right), with these home-made feeders. —*Vanessa Mow*
Farmington, Pennsylvania

Through trial and error we've discovered the best place for our bird feeders is approximately 10 feet away from the house. The distance keeps squirrels from using our roof as a launch pad, yet it's not too far for us to shovel a path to the feeders in winter. And we get a great view from our windows.

—*Dale and Ardis Amundson*
Cumberland, Wisconsin

I go to auto salvage yards to find smooth hubcaps to use as squirrel baffles. I drill a hole in the hubcaps, slide them onto the pole and hold them in place with a hose clamp. When squirrels grab the hubcap, it tilts and the squirrel falls to the ground. —*Bill Scheiblein*
New Port Richey, Florida

Barbara Dunn

To attract more bluebirds (above), be sure to space your nest boxes 50 to 100 feet apart.

—*Tony Sowers, Milo, Iowa*

We've had amazing success attracting hummingbirds after we planted *Salvia greggii*, a sage that's covered with small pink flowers.

—*Karin Arrigoni*
San Jose, California

I collect leftover cooking grease all summer long in coffee cans, so I have plenty to use as suet for birds in winter. Just pour the fat into the cans after you cook and store them in the freezer. Between layers of grease, I'll add cranberries, birdseed, nuts… just about any healthy food will work. I serve the treat to birds in a mesh bag during winter.

—*Jonell Lening, Lamar, Colorado*

Here's a list of ingredients you might want to mix in with your next batch of homemade bird treats: Cereal, leftover ground meat, nuts, dry dog food or dog treats, popcorn, hamster pellets, grape jelly, graham crackers, peanut butter or cornmeal.

They all seem to draw feathered friends to our backyard.

—*Elaine Mobley*
East Freedom, Pennsylvania

I enjoy making suet for my backyard birds, but it's pretty messy. So I came up with this method to make the process neater—spoon the suet into resealable sandwich bags and form it into a shape that fits your feeder. Then store it in the freezer until you need a refill. Your hands will stay clean. —*Alice Jester*
Baltimore, Maryland

Beef suet gives birds energy to generate warmth during winter's coldest months. Most butcher shops will sell or give it away. I always run the suet through a meat grinder, then melt it on the stove to make pure white "energy blocks".

—*Elaine Mobley*
East Freedom, Pennsylvania

Birds love special treats—especially my birdseed cookies. Follow any suet recipe and use bird-shaped cookie cutters to create individual servings. Hang them from tree branches using heavy string.

—*Lynn Sovel*
Sand Springs, Oklahoma

I add stale pancake mix to my homemade suet. I like to try different mixtures, so I never follow the same suet recipe. But since adding the mix, I've attracted lots more birds. —*Nancy Black Yorktown, Virginia*

When I make jelly (like grape or elderberry) that needs to be strained through cheesecloth, I save the leftovers in resealable bags and freeze them. Then when I make homemade suet, I add this secret ingredient. The birds love it. —*Lois Minosky Zanesville, Ohio*

Homemade pie dough is a favorite of woodpeckers, nuthatches and chickadees. In fact, I whip up a special batch just for them. Here's the recipe:

Use any pie dough recipe and add peanut butter, nuts and seeds. I sometimes include dog food (a good source of protein) and meat drippings.

When finished, roll the mixture into balls and place in onion bags.

During warm weather, the balls will melt, so be sure to hang it where it won't leave a greasy mess.

—*Joyce LaBelle Onaway, Michigan*

If you have a suet recipe that hardens well, form it into doughnut shapes and tie a string through the middle so you can hang the offerings from trees in your yard. It's an easy way to provide the birds' favorite treat. —*Brenda Haley Thorsby, Alberta*

Collect the drippings from summer cookouts and use them for making suet for the birds.

Melt the fat, pour it into tuna or cat food cans and stir in chopped oranges, raisins, sunflower seeds and peanuts. Then store in the refrigerator until needed.

Woodpeckers really go for this high-energy food—especially in winter. —*Beverly Davis Ballston Spa, New York*

Since we've started mixing our own birdseed, we've had fewer house sparrows (below) at our feeders. Here's the simple recipe:

Mix 3 parts black-oil sunflower seeds, 2 parts striped sunflower

seeds, 1-1/2 parts white millet and 1 part safflower seed.

You'll enjoy the results as much as the birds you want attract do.

—*Luci Laughlin Fort Wayne, Indiana*

Cooked spaghetti looks a lot like mealworms, which is why I think my backyard birds love the soft noodles. I cook up about a cup of the pasta, then add a little peanut butter and bacon grease to it before cutting into 1-inch segments. —*Pat Stark Nevada, Missouri*

Suet treats are easy to handle when you freeze them in plastic wrap. Just drop a couple spoonfuls onto a piece of wrap, fold the edges and freeze. Your hands stay clean when you unwrap it. Just drop the treat into empty suet cages. No mess!
—*Lola Fields, Wesley, Arkansas*

Northern cardinals (that's a male above) can't resist my seed mix. Combine peanuts, sunflower seeds, millet and corn and serve on a tray feeder. They love it!
—*Wendy Ruprecht*
Cold Spring, Minnesota

Prepare a standard fruitcake recipe and hollow out the center (enjoy it yourself or place it on a tray feeder for the birds).

Then mix sunflower seeds into warm suet and let it cool. While it's still pliable, spoon the concoction into the fruitcake cavity and let it set in the refrigerator until hardened.

All backyard birds love this treat, especially blue jays and nuthatches.
—*Rose Kachuk*
Clearwater, British Columbia

Spread mixed birdseed, sunflower hearts and peanuts on a greased pan. Then fill a spray bottle with liquid unflavored gelatin, applying enough of the mixture to dampen the seed. Refrigerate until hardened, cut into squares and place in suet feeders. I've found this recipe holds up best in cold weather.
—*Sharon DeBruin, Gowrie, Iowa*

I serve crushed eggshells to birds. They're an excellent source of calcium.

To do this, rinse and dry the shells and bake on a cookie sheet at 250° until the edges begin to brown. Baking the shells helps kill any bacteria.
—*Carol Van Norman*
Swartz Creek, Michigan

The secret ingredient in my successful suet recipe is cheese! I melt suet, then add American cheese, millet, bread crumbs and a little sand for grit. I pour the mixture into empty tuna cans and serve to the birds.
—*Ann Sturgeon*
Kokomo, Indiana

By George…A squirrel's natural diet consists of nuts, fruits, berries, mushrooms and insects. Many suburban backyards offer a similar natural habitat, with the added bonus of an abundance of bird food.
—*George Harrison*
Contributing Editor
Source: Squirrel Wars

Mix Cheerios cereal and inexpensive broken nuts (I prefer peanuts or cashews) with sunflower seeds. A huge variety of birds go crazy over this mix.

—*Deborah Fluharty*
Coraopolis, Pennsylvania

If you have leftover or outdated canned dog food, don't toss it. Make this recipe that is sure to have birds flocking to your backyard:

2 cups freshly ground suet
1 can (14 oz.) moist dog food

Melt suet and stir in dog food. Let cook for 10 minutes until mixture is slightly liquid. Fill plastic containers and chill. Place mix in suet cages or in a suet bag.

—*Gloria Meredith*
Harrington, Delaware

Use a muffin tin lined with paper baking cups to form suet cakes. They fit nicely into my suet feeder and the paper cups keep my hands clean as I fill it.   —*S.D. Valentine*
South Hadley, Massachusetts

Keep a resealable food storage bag in your cupboard and collect dry food scraps for the birds. I mix broken potato chips, stale cereal and cookies. When you have a few extra minutes, add some melted peanut butter or lard to the mix and serve to birds on a tray feeder.

—*Karen Sanderson-Buschow*
Pemberton, Minnesota

Skim off grease as you're cooking meals and add it to a container that you keep in the refrigerator. You

Lois Nielswander

IT'S A FACT...

Owls are the only birds with forward-looking eyes that work like a human's do. Because both eyes operate together, they have "binocular" vision that's truly three-dimensional. This makes it easier for these birds of prey to hunt.

can add birdseed, oatmeal or nuts between layers. When your container is full, remove the mix and set it outside for the birds to enjoy.

—*Gay Haefner, Shawnee, Kansas*

After frying bacon, pork chops and other meat products, I carefully pour the leftover grease into a bowl lined with waxed paper and stir in some birdseed. Then I put it in the freezer.

Once it's solid, peel off the waxed paper and place the special snack in a suet feeder. It's the quickest way I know to make the birds a homemade treat.   —*Kim Bryant*
Carlton, Minnesota

The Last Word from George

Since beef suet adds fat to birds' diets to keep them warm, is it unhealthy to offer it in a tropical climate? —Cheryl Christofferson
Lake Worth, Florida

George: No. Fat produces energy, which is converted to body heat, so it's a necessary part of all birds' diets. Beef suet is more nutritious for birds than ordinary fat, but it can melt in hot weather. Suet mixed with a binder, like cornmeal or nuts, offers better hot-weather bird food.

THERE'S NO SUBSTITUTE for experience. That's why we're happy to have Contributing Editor George Harrison on our staff.

Besides enjoying the hobby for his entire life, he's a respected authority on backyard birding.

George shared so many great backyard birding tips and answers to questions from *Birds & Blooms* readers for this book, we didn't want to leave any out.

So here are a few extra for you to try in your backyard—before you know it, you'll have a bird haven as active as George's.

If hummingbirds are ignoring the blooms in your special hummingbird garden, try placing a nectar feeder nearby.

Create your own backyard "field guide" by taking photos of the birds you see at your feeders and keep them in a scrapbook. This also is a good place to include your birding "life list".

Although some people think collecting bird nests would make an interesting hobby, federal law protects the nests, so it's illegal to collect them.

Here are some solutions if crows have taken over your backyard bird haven:
• Eliminate suet feeders or use a seed feeder with small or no perches at all.
• Use a weight-sensitive feeder. Its feeding port closes when a large bird (or critter) lands on its perch.
• Offer only safflower seed in your feeders.
• Enclose feeders in wire mesh.

To keep larger birds from raiding your hummingbird feeders, purchase one without perches or try a feeder with only a single feeding tube extending from the reservoir.

Is there birdseed that sparrows won't eat? I use mixed birdseed, and the sparrows eat it all and scare away the other birds.
—Mrs. John Wheeler, Rigby, Idaho

George: Sparrows love most of the ingredients in wild birdseed mixes. The solution is to offer seed that sparrows don't like, such as niger, safflower and sunflower in the shell (though some house sparrows are able to crack sunflower shells).

Also, sparrows usually can't feed from tube feeders without perches. Unfortunately, the same is true for northern cardinals.

George Harrison

Recovery time for birds that have stunned themselves by flying into windows can range from a few minutes to more than an hour. You may want to cover them with a kitchen sieve or colander to protect them from predators while they're in this vulnerable state (see photo above). Once the bird begins to recover, allow it to retreat to the safety of a nearby tree or shrub.

To help get through cold winter nights, chickadees, titmice and nuthatches often disappear into an abandoned woodpecker nesting cavity, or perhaps into the same cavity or nest box in which they were raised.

We like to feed suet cakes to our backyard birds, but the blackbirds get to it first. How can we keep them away?
—Debby Heinz Bellbrook, Ohio

George: The best way to keep blackbirds—and starlings—from eating suet is to place the suet feeder inside a larger mesh enclosure with openings big enough that smaller birds can get through, but small enough to exclude pesky ones. Another possibility is hanging the suet feeder under a squirrel baffle. Blackbirds are uncomfortable if they have to hang while eating.

"Bully birds" are often attracted to seeds that drop from feeders. But you can stop them by placing a deep container—like a garbage can—below the feeder to collect the cast-off seeds. Most birds won't fly into such a deep basin.

Woodpeckers peck on houses to announce their presence to potential mates, declare their territory in spring or search for roosting sites in winter.

You can discourage them by putting mylar balloons, aluminum pie pans, strips of aluminum foil or Christmas tree tinsel near their favorite pecking spots.

Index